W.R.E.a.C Havoc Enterprises
presents...

JUST MY THOUGHTS, LADIES AND GENTLEMEN

A collection of short stories and poetry by Jamiyl Samuels

DEDICATION

Thank you God for blessing me with the ability to create and write my thoughts on paper and allowing me the platform to share with the world.

My work is dedicated to my wife Tracy-Ann, my son Trey Amani, and daughter Aja Emily: as always I love you guys. Thank you for continuing to inspire and drive me to be the best husband, father, and person.

Thank you to my mom Vilma, my sister Andrea, my Uncle Barry and my entire family for your endless support and promotion of my writing.

My partner in rhyme Abdul Naim Rivera, p.k.a Bleek-oner b.k.a GStakmillz, the *"Rhyme Finatic"* chapter is dedicated to you and all those who have supported my music career in the past. Styles May Vary will return! N.U.T.S crew!

To those who support my work and follow my blog whether you know me or not, God bless you. You make what I do that much more special to me and a privilege I will not take for granted.

R.I.P.

Clifford "Boisy" Samuels, Sr.
1946-2013
Douglas Lyall Lewis, Sr.
1947-2014

Other books by Jamiyl Samuels &
W.R.E.a.C Havoc Publishing:

*Pass The Torch: How A Young Black Father
Challenges The 'Deadbeat Dad' Stereotype*

*Available at Createspace.com e-store(www.createspace.com/5963484),
Amazon.com, Barnesandnoble.com, and other online retail outlets.*

The Amazing Adventures of Awesome Amani

*Available at Createspace.com e-store (www.createspace.com/5002485),
Amazon.com, Barnesandnoble.com, and other online retail outlets.*

Coming Soon…

Partners

The Black Sheep.

Follow Jamiyl Samuels:
Facebook *jamiylsamuels*
Twitter @*wreachavocwritr*
Instagram *jamiylwrites*

TABLE OF CONTENTS

DON'T BE AFRAID TO BE GREAT

a waste of TIME

Being locked up is no joke… I realize
that now…

now that my future is a thing of the
past… I think of all the civilians I
harassed after being gassed/

by so-called friends I thought had my
back but when I got caught hauled ass

niggas that I thought were my right
hand took flight, man/ the long arm of
the law can't take 'em light, fam or
you'll find yourself facing indictment

niggas I called brothers, Blood - but
not really/ just a color, not Celie/

no purple just yellow/ down the spines
of these cats whose hearts pump jello

when I was a young fellow sold me the
dream of being down with a team/

but I had to plot and scheme on
innocent people to get the cream

when I coulda just got a job - they
schooled me on how to rob - now life
ain't worth 50 cent now that I'm
sentenced

cuz y'all still chillin' in the town
while I'm rockin' these browns/

y'all still knockin' freaks down while
I'm chillin' wit clowns

asking me what I'm jacking - my freedom
- and the life I want back and/

 interaction with my real family
shoulda given me satisfaction/ but I
wanted a piece of the action

now I gotta throw hands over cookies,
being called a rookie like jail is some
kind of sport/ but none of these niggas
is LeBron on the court

the only one I'ma see is Brooklyn
Supreme/ my life in the hands of a
judge named Rabin I coulda been
chillin' wit Raheem...

but I got the juice now, right?

Instead of hanging out nights I'm
locked in at 10/ gotta be told where
and when by CO's in the pen

strip searched and told when to bend –
and cough/ jacking my dick to get a nut
off/ ain't this a bitch get that slut
off

this ain't life but I'm facing it - if
you were me you'd want a replacement/

it's the concrete jungle and you ain't
built for the pavement...

on top of that I gotta go to school/ I
ain't go on the outside but here it's
the rule

I pity the fool who knock on my cell/
6:30 in the morning I'ma set off the
bells/

I'm thinking 'bout bail, getting out of
this hell

this I never envisioned/ I just had my
girl in this position how I get in this
position?

I'm in jail but been in mental prison

can I blame it on no father? Why
bother? My other homey had no dad
graduated with honors

I blame being a follower I bust a rhyme
for my leaders/ pitchin' is a short
stop no Jeter

no home cookin' I'm missing food in the
worst way/ can't mess with turkey stew,
chicken Sunday and Thursday

missing out on my birthday trying to
get that cake/ thinking I'm keeping it
real wit niggas that's fake/ I get my
hands on 'em they'll be planning a wake

my life's at stake for swinging a
hammer/ like a hood Thor my mind's
racing brain's in a figure four

coulda been the first in my family to
see college/

it ain't a victory to have a degree in
street knowledge

I ain't trying to preach cuz I ain't break the cycle/

don't point to a priest don't hand me a Bible/ cuz I'll just use it for my phone numbers...

at least I ain't in a mod still the stress is killing me/

cuz I keep to myself niggas is ice grilling me/

I ain't wit all the talking trying to get a rep wit violence/

if these niggas know the streets real niggas move in silence

so I'll lock in before 2:30 I'm reading before 9/

while niggas just starting to chef trying to get extra time/

talking bout they HKA but ain't never swept the tier/

trying to be S.P.A. but ain't none certified here

I spend my days wisely run out to law library/ keep a fresh cut never miss commissary/

good looking out mom I know I made you mad/ I embarrassed the family made the neighbors gossip, my bad

but you still came through hopefully I can rise above/

get a second chance on the street so I can return the love

just a victim of bad choices you know most of us are/ showing off in front of the fellas don't make you a star/

just a book and case number now I'm on the radar/

it's like no matter how far away you go you can't stray far

it's like can I be mad now if I'm profiled and shit/

or pulled over in my ride for a stop and frisk/

I can't let this jail mentality consume me/ I can't let my failed reality ruin me

you know why? My lady came to see me I got a v-i-/

she ain't a mule she ain't bringing shit to get me high/

but she got me touching the sky cuz
what she said to me lately/ I'm gonna
be a father she expecting a baby…

Damn… I gotta get outta here, man…

WHAM BAMM!!

"Jay! Jaaaaaayyy!!"

Damn.

That is the familiar voice of my mother calling me when she wants me to run an errand.

"Come go to the store and get some beans to put in the ox-tail for me".

Damn.

Usually I would honor this simple request without hesitation. However, Mother decides to ask me this favor after I take off all my clothes and get comfortable in the middle of my NBA2K11 season. I'm killing the Chicago Bulls with the New York Knicks. They can't stop Stoudamire.

"Stoudamire stuffs it home!" yells the announcer in the same excitement I was feeling before...

"Jaylen!"

I immediately jump up this time. Whenever a parent calls you by your full name, you're usually in trouble. I turn off my television, but I leave the Xbox 360 on (I do not want to replay this game). I reluctantly throw on the clothes I just took off and head downstairs to meet my mother, who is holding the money with a smile that says: "I would go, but since you're home..."

I can't help but smile as I turn towards the door. Sure the store is a block and a half away, but having to go there at this time is messing up my routine.

I step outside to a wind that hits me in the face like a Mike Tyson right hook circa 1988. I am immediately reminded why I did not want to come back out here and I have a sneaking suspicion that is why my mother did not want to come out here either.

While locking the door I decide that it is useless to pout. The faster

I get to the store, the faster I come back home and continue pounding the Bulls, my way of taking out the frustration for all those years in the '90s Michael Jordan beat the Knicks in the playoffs.

"Splash!" "One three pointer from Carmelo Anthony for Game 7 of the 1992 semifinals."

"Arrggh!" "One slam for Charles Smith's inability to utilize his 6'10" frame to do just that in Game 5 of the 1993 Eastern Conference Finals."

I was just a little bitter.

My speed walking skills allow me to walk a block and a half in less than 30 seconds (I could have run, but I do not feel this trip warrants wearing myself out). I reach my destination, Ricardo's Deli, and walk in. Strangely enough I have never been in this place before, but I have passed it many a time on my way to the supermarket only two blocks up the street. There was no reason to choose today as my first time patronizing the store, except for the fact that two blocks less to walk was ideal for someone with a game on extended pause.

I make eye contact with who I assume is Ricardo since he is behind the counter and keep it moving, disregarding his 'young Black man' stereotypical glances. The look he gave me only means that people that look like me frequent this deli and most likely have not always been friendly.

The place is divided by a huge shelf that stretches throughout the length of the store leaving room to maneuver to both sides of it. I made my way to the side away from the counter and out of Ricardo's view. There is another shelf filled with produce against the wall of the store which extends the same distance, but there's no maneuvering around this shelf unless you want to go through the wall.

Making my way down the aisle I look to my left and right scanning the shelves in search of the canned goods. At the middle of the aisle my forward motion is impeded by a small, thin woman who – interestingly enough – gives me the same look as Ricardo. This from a customer in the store! I was growing increasingly uncomfortable at this point.

"How are you doing?" I say to the woman, my voice dripping with sarcasm.

I make my way around the patron and spot the beans. I grab the object of my search and circle back around. I stop at the sight of a little cat (virtually every bodega has one) walking towards me. Before I bend down to make silly faces at the critter, I notice another young man in a huge winter coat walk in. I didn't think anything of the fact that this guy had both hands in his pocket and the coat's hood over his head, a baseball cap protruding out ever so slightly.

I bend down to play with the cat: "hey buddy, bjui buji boo boo (I talk to cats like they are babies)." The slim woman is standing a few yards away from me. I can feel her watching me like I am some sort of psycho. She should have been watching the character that just walked into the store, I thought. At least she could see my body parts. That guy was buried inside the coat he was wearing.

"Gimme all the money in the register!"

My brow furrowed. Maybe Ricardo just turned up the volume on a television he had behind the counter.

"Am I speaking French , muthafucka?! Put all the money in the bag!"

I slowly rise to the tips of my feet, using every inch of my six-foot frame to quietly peek over the aisle divider and see what was happening.

At that moment the cat takes off for the back room.

"Coward," I whisper.

I suddenly come to the realization that I am a witness to a stick-up. The gunman looked about 5'7" to 5'9" in height and no older than 17. These are the features of the typical young Black male. I begin to understand why I got looked at like I had a bomb strapped to my chest when I entered the store.

Mental note: Stay away from Ricardo's.

"Hurry up!" the gunman yells.

His right arm is pointing a 9mm pistol at the skull of Ricardo as he nervously watches Ricardo stuff the bag.

"Okay my friend, take it easy," reasons Ricardo.

"Muthafucka I ain't yo' friend," the young man shouts as he looks toward the door.

At the same moment, someone who was about to enter the store wisely passes on the thought. Seeing he was witnessed, the gunman gets a little antsy.

"Come on! I'll blast you!"

Damn. I don't wanna see that. I look down the aisle at the other unfortunate witness to what may be a homicide.

'I left my Xbox for this?' I thought to myself.

I'm too young to be a witness to a crime, or worse yet a victim. I watch the other woman slowly easing her way to the end of the aisle until she is parallel to where the gunman is standing. With four incredible shoves of each section of the shelves, her petite, slim-frame sent a mountain of beverages, laundry detergent, huge bags of cat and dog food, you name it, tumbling down on top of the crook in a fantastic landslide.

"WHAM! BAM!"

That was the sound of the heaviest items in the store thundering down on this kid. His weapon, dislodged from his hand upon impact, was quickly pounced on by Ricardo who looked like Edwin Moses the way he hurdled the counter.

Needless to say I was stunned. Where did this small woman find all of that strength? Was the kid still alive under the inventory that fell on him? I was shocked to see the other witness run to Ricardo's side and smothered him with hugs and kisses.

She was really friendly for a customer. Turns out she was no customer at all, but Ricardo's wife. She was watching me the same reason Ricardo was. This husband and wife tandem was really a team. I guess I looked suspicious enough to garner the double team effect, an effort only an owner besieged by multiple robberies can implement. Once I got out of eye sight of Ricardo, his wife took over as security.

After the initial shock of what just happened wore off, I had to say I was mildly impressed by the team work of this couple. Was that shelf strategically placed to be used as a weapon on would be criminals? I was giving them too much credit now. I could have thrown my can of beans at the kid and had the same effect.

Okay, probably not.

My deep intellectual thought was interrupted by the sound of police sirens in the distance. I quickly made my way towards the shocked couple.

"I'm alright chica," Ricardo reassured his frantic wife who continued to smother him with kisses.

I kept my eyes to the door when I noticed through my peripheral vision that Ricardo was looking at me. I made eye contact with him.

"We're not all like that," I said.

At the same time I pulled out a dollar bill to pay for the beans. Ricardo did not reach for it so I let it drop to the floor. I took one last look at the buried perpetrator and shook my head.

"What a way to go out," I thought.

He'd get laughed out of the business. I can imagine the conversation in prison:

"What are you in for?"

"Robbery."

"How'd they catch you?"

"They pushed a shelf over on me. I got buried alive in food."

"OK, who wants to pound him first?"

As the sirens grew louder I high-tailed it out of that store knowing a trip to the police station would further delay my domination of the Chicago Bulls.

I WANT YOU BACK

The late Michael Jackson.

It feels weird typing it…reading it, let alone saying it.

The consummate entertainer, my boyhood (and adult) idol was no more. He was only 20 years and 3 days older than I was. I always took pride in the fact that we had the same astrological sign: Virgo. Although I was never into astrology it was a link, however miniscule, to a superstar I only met through television, video, and records. I knew once Michael's birthday rolled around on August 29th I was three days away from turning a year older.

Gone too soon.

I still remember what I was doing when I heard the tragic news. The stunned silence, my stomach felt as if I was in the midst of the first big drop on a rollercoaster. My mouth agape in disbelief I stared at the television tuned to E! News hoping it was a horrible rumor like the ones that plagued the King of Pop the last 20 years of his life.

It was not a rumor. The incomparable man-child, the six year old dynamo with the voice of gold on *"Big Boy"*, the 11-year old with the swagger of a man three times his age that gave us stirring renditions of soon to be classics hits like *"Who's Loving You"*, *"I Want You Back"* (sung equally as brilliant by *David Ruffin* – without backup singers), and others.

Who could forget the sound of gliding piano keys immediately followed by an ongoing guitar lick and intermittent bassline that served as the official genesis of a legendary career?

The year: 1969.

Although it was nine years before I was born, whenever I drop the needle on the old 45 (record), play the CD, or push play on my iPod, "I Want You Back", the ad-libs of the pint sized lead singer filled with the excitement only a debut single on a world famous Motown label can bring, fills me with joy.

A quick search of YouTube lists numerous variety shows where the number 1 single was performed: *The Ed Sullivan Show*, *The Hollywood Palace*, *Sonny and Cher's* show to name a few. It was through these clips I witnessed the incomparable Jackson 5 choreography. There they were, five brothers their outfits as much a statement of who they were as the songs, a kaleidoscope of color as monochromatic as their logo.

With older brothers Jackie and Marlon to his right, Michael joined them throwing his arms to the sky before quickly pulling them down across his chest as he dipped low, his legs crossed, beginning a slow turn. With their back to the audience first Marlon, then Jackie and finally Michael spun back around and posed for the audience. Kick steps and hand shuffles follow, the other two brothers Tito and Jermaine - guitars in hand - effortlessly imitate the moves with their lower bodies, before Michael grabs the microphone.

At this point I used to fancy myself a makeshift DJ on my CD player, pushing the rewind button right before Michael starts the first verse. If I timed it right, the piano loop would begin again, after a slight pause, without missing a beat.

The 14-year old, voice slightly altered by puberty, singing an emotional tribute to a rat (*"Ben"*), possibly foreshadowing his love/obsession with exotic animals, the 16-year old debuting "The Robot" dance move with the disco themed "Dancing Machine", the month of his 21st birthday, releasing *"Off The Wall"* to the masses cementing his emancipation from his brothers. Who could forget that smile on the cover artwork? The black tuxedo, soon-to-be signature white socks glowing, perfectly picked afro, the last time his visage would be free from surgery.

Then in December of 1982 it happened.

The release of what would be the biggest selling album of all time. No one at the time could have known except the man himself. Reportedly miffed at a poor showing at the Grammys for "Off

The Wall", Jackson set out to outdo his Epic debut. To say "Thriller" surpassed "Off The Wall" would be a colossal understatement. It only contained nine songs, an EP by today's standards, a full length masterpiece at that time and now.

"Thriller", "Billie Jean", "Beat It", "Human Nature", "The Girl Is Mine". Every song could have been a single. The accompanying videos forced rock-themed (to put it nicely) MTV to play this Black man's mini-movies on their network.

I still remember his show stopping performance on "Motown 25: Yesterday, Today, Forever" even though I was only four years old when it premiered in May of 1983. Forget, for a second, that it was the first time Michael and his brothers had shared the stage together as The Jackson 5 in seven years. Wearing a glistening black jacket (later revealed to be his mother's) to match his shirt, The Glove, and his socks, Michael stood out.

I am not sure how much I understood about what was taking place because obviously I never saw them perform as The Jackson 5. I really only knew

Michael from the "Billie Jean" video. When he completed the set with his brothers and they left the stage I did not know what to expect. When he pulled out the black Fedora it seemed out of his back pocket I went crazy as the familiar drums began to "Billie Jean". The moves were like nothing I had ever seen: the timely pelvic thrusts, the leg-kick into a turn, another leg-kick and back facing the crowd, then the Fedora came off, thrown into a crowd of rabid fans to be ripped to shreds.

Poor Fedora.

But this was the magic of Michael Jackson. What his pre-pubescent vocals did in the 70's, his improved choreography added another tool to his arsenal. He was lip-synching, but who cared? You already knew he could sing. The dance moves were the story. But he wasn't done. At the breakdown he stepped to the right of the stage and pumped a finger at the crowd "Hee!" He stepped to the left of the stage and pumped a finger at that side of the crowd "Whoo!" Then the hand extended. He looked left then right. At this point you were wondering what was going to happen next.

Then the thought was answered as Jackson started to glide backward across the stage.

Where were you when Michael unveiled "The Moonwalk"?

That question has been placed in the American lexicon with other great and tragic moments in history: Neil Armstrong walking on the moon, the assassination of JFK, Martin Luther King, Jr. and Malcolm X, the election of Barack Obama as President of the United States, among others.

It was his greatest moment to that point. It sent him into the stratosphere and I witnessed it. No one could tell me anything about Michael after that. I remember pulling out the illustrated poster of Michael from the New York Daily News (along with Prince, Madonna, and Tina Turner) and hanging it on my wall. To think he didn't go on his own tour until "Bad" was released, yet songs from "Thriller" and "Off The Wall" dominated the "Victory" tour concerts with his brothers.

I think of the screaming fans passing out at his concerts and say there is no way I would pay thousands of dollars for a front row seat just to pass out minutes into the show and get carried out of the arena. Then again I totally lost my mind when Jay-Z brought Michael out on stage during a summer concert in 2001. I want to say I went crazy because it was totally unexpected that he would appear. Jay-Z was on top of the rap world at the time, but he couldn't possibly know Michael Jackson like that. Michael was other worldly. When Jay called for Michael a second time and he didn't appear I kinda thought he was frontin'.

"I know he better get out here", Jay beckoned.

I saw a slight figure come from the right side of the stage. I was too far back to see, but from the reaction of the people in the front row I knew it was him. A look at one of the big screens confirmed it. The only time I ever saw Michael Jackson in person.

I am a true fan. When his skin started changing color I noticed. How could you not. The cover art of "Bad" is dramatically different from "Thriller", dramatically different from how he looked in the "We Are the World" clip. It was undeniable: the straightened nose, the guy-liner, and of course the white skin. I saw that his features were altered by the disease that is plastic surgery addiction. He said it was a skin disease, many said he was bleaching his skin, that he didn't want to be Black. I even bought into a rumor that he was so in love with Diana Ross that, since she only dated and married White men, he wanted to look White so she would miraculously want him.

I knew he was teased as a kid, called "tomato nose" among other things by his brothers. I wish he had never broken his nose doing what he does best. His first surgery to correct the break allegedly began a destructive cycle of repeated nose jobs. All in all his music was all that mattered. Just keep making music.

I watched his public service announcement in 1993 in defense of child abuse charges. He was innocent, I believed. But as he settled that case and went to court to fight two others I got angry. Not for people to leave Michael alone - all stars are criticized by the media it comes with the territory in a sense, I guess. No. I wished Michael wasn't so child-like.

That way he would not be such an easy target for these people to call him a predator.

He said he missed out on his childhood, but so did his brothers. Not to sound insensitive, but it is frustrating that someone with such enormous talent and a gift to pull on the heart strings of millions of people worldwide, the power to bring people together through music and dance was brought down by something so juvenile.

They dissected his sex life. Why couldn't he enjoy the groupies like his brothers? They say losing your virginity changes a man, puts some hair on his chest so to speak. Maybe he would have been a different person.

Then again, that is selfish of me. Michael turned away from the multitude of women on those early tours because of his religious beliefs. The beliefs instilled in him by his beloved mother Katherine. Can't knock him for that.

God knows what He is doing. He sent Michael Jackson to try to heal the world in the face of enormous hate and vicious slander of his own character. As his brother Marlon said at his very public funeral: "maybe now they'll leave you alone". But why did it have to come to that?

I am sure now that Michael is gone many of the people that criticized him, ridiculed him, and mocked him were some of the same people crying. That is the hypocrisy of the human race we live in. Build someone up to tear them down only to praise them and their work when they pass on. I am satisfied knowing that ultimately I never reduced myself to piling on when his star faded.

In Michael's death I have found out more about his life. How he allegedly staged pictures of him "sleeping" in a hyperbaric chamber to get people talking. I am sure he never imagined he would need little staging to get the media talking about him once the decade turned to the 1990s.

He went from "Artist of the Decade" to "Wacko Jacko". His bad press was overshadowing his music, which was still potent through the mid '90s. How ironic a man that so often sang about world peace and brotherly love was so tormented by the very humanity he tried to save.

Who knew the sixth take (?!) of a Pepsi commercial would start Michael's downfall? Why did they need all those takes for that stupid commercial anyway?? The third take looked fine to me. Who was working the pyrotechnics? Why would they set it off and the man was still at the top of the stairs?

The burned scalp Michael suffered during the shooting of this Pepsi commercial allegedly led to the addiction to prescription drugs that would lead to the subsequent abuse of medication that would kill him, or have him killed.

I listen to his songs, I see clips of the Jacksons variety show online and I shake my head. Why didn't Michael stay the way he was? What did Joe really do to him?

Even though Michael said it did not matter if you were Black or White I choose to remember him when his skin was a beautiful brown hue. Am I wrong for that?

I take comfort in knowing that Michael is somewhere where the tabloids can't affect him, another doctor can't prescribe him medication or alter him surgically. There can be nothing else to say about his physical features, his bank account, how he treats kids, if he was really the biological father of his kids, whether he was gay, or did he have any of his nose left. It was as if people forgot who this man was and how he changed - no, **saved** the music industry at one point.

I have not forgotten and I will never forget Michael Jackson as long as I live.

Rest in Peace, King.

*FREESTYLE FRIDAY

*THIS STORY IS BASED ON ACTUAL EVENTS FROM A LIVE TAPING OF BET'S 106 AND PARK FREESTYLE FRIDAY SEGMENT ON MARCH 16TH 2001. ALL NAMES ARE OF REAL PEOPLE PRESENT DURING THIS MEMORABLE COMPETITION.

I walked briskly down Park Avenue because I knew the line would be long to get in. March 16th 2001 started out like any other day for me. I made my way to class at Long Island University's Brooklyn campus. It was an important time for me for within two short months I would be receiving my Bachelor's degree in English. However, I spent the day anticipating where I was going and what I would be doing that afternoon.

I was a 22 year-old aspiring Hip Hop artist who would be making his first nationally televised appearance on Black Entertainment Television or BET for short. Dressed in a black and gray sweater with interlocking "RW"'s along the chest and sleeves, black jeans, a matching black jeans jacket, and a black cap with the New York Mets "NY" logo in blue and black stitch in the center, I made sure I looked the part.

A quick check of the street sign above me said I was on East 106th street. As I turned left down the block, I noticed the huge line of youngsters waiting to get into the building. They were cordoned off by a long black stanchion. Two men in all-black suits with muscular frames stood at the entrance of the building.

As I walked toward the end of the line, I could feel numerous sets of eyes watching me. Through my peripheral vision I noticed the youths looking me up and down. The crowd was decidedly of the teenage variety as is the demographic that watches the music video show about to be taped in half an hour. I was a fan of the show, but I was really in attendance to perform in the freestyle rap battle segment that aired every Friday.

'This would be big for my budding rap career,' I thought. Millions of people watch the show. Imagine if I won.

This was the second time I was at this show. A week earlier I sat in the audience for the first time. The day had added meaning as it was the fourth anniversary of the death of Brooklyn Hip Hop legend The Notorious B.I.G., and I had been hoping to be picked to perform in the rap battle, but it was not to be. It would have been great for me to be able to represent Brooklyn for the man who did it faithfully until his untimely death in 1997.

If there was a positive to be taken from the missed opportunity it was that I got a chance to see what I could expect. I was able to take in the atmosphere and to size up the competition for the following week. A rapper named Illa Danz from New Jersey took the stage against a taller adversary. This would be the first battle for Danz. A sign that said "Challenger" hung around his neck. The other guy was the "Champion"(and I use the term loosely) for the moment.

Illa Danz was the shorter guy, but he had a big voice. Once the music came on he went into attack mode. With demonstrative hand movements and witty wordplay, Danz got the crowd going. The competition was none. There was a reason I couldn't remember anything more than that the guy was tall. He was barely audible, struggled putting his words together before finally stopping short of his 30 second time limit.

I might have missed the week when this guy became champion, but I was curious to know how it happened. He looked far from championship material. So the stage was set. It would be me against the champion Illa Danz.

At the end of the line I survey the kids that moments ago made me the center of attention. I periodically looked off to the right at empty air space filled with nervous energy. Young people are hard to please. I wondered how they would receive me on stage. Would Illa Danz embarrass me like his opponent the week before?

"Please have your ID's out with your reservation!" yells a woman dressed in a white T-shirt and khaki pants.

She checks the paperwork, a copy of the e-mail they sent confirming that you are a member of the audience for the specific taping, and ID cards of the youngsters in line with the information she has on the clipboard she is holding in her hand. As the line begins moving I feel a tingle in my stomach.

When I finally get inside I am met by a metal detector placed at the outskirts of what seems to be a waiting room. Inside the room the long tables on wheels give off the feeling of being in a cafeteria. Each person is given a piece of paper upon entrance into the waiting room. The paper is a release form that has to be signed by everyone in order to be placed in the studio audience. I put my John Hancock on the form and waited patiently, occasionally surveying the flock of boisterous teens scattered around the room. Some were on cell phones, some wearing blue bandanas and outerwear.

I turned my attention back to the security station. I notice a tall, husky brother enter the room in a black suit. His head is shaved clean. I learn later that he is affectionately called "Big Head" by the hosts.

"Listen up!" he shouts.

The commotion calms to a smattering of whispers.

"We're gonna be taking you upstairs in a minute, but first there are rules."

I heard this last week. I turn my attention to the floor and start bopping my head to imaginary music which is normal for me. I always hear music. I had dreams of playing the drums and guitar that have yet to be realized.

"All cell phones, pagers, 2-way's must be turned completely off," the guard continues. "If I hear a phone, it's mine."

A few kids chuckle, but this guy is dead serious. If he was joking I wasn't going to be the one to find out.

"There is to be no gum chewing. If I see you chewing, you can do one of two things: you can swallow it, or … 106th street."

This drew laughter from the room. 106th street meant being kicked out, standing on the actual street. I smiled to myself. That was a clever way of putting it.

"There are to be no gang signs made in the camera. If I see you moving fingers … 106th street."

At this point the Bloods and Crips gang culture that invaded New York in the late 90's was in full force. These same teenagers in the room with me were the same age of the knuckleheads committing violent petty crimes against unsuspecting citizens and babies (I heard a disturbing story that a baby was slashed by one of those cowards because he had a red coat on) to be "down".

My thing is if you are going to co-opt an organized culture from the West Coast, at least know the meaning and history behind what you are doing. Don't just throw on the colors and think you are certified. A lot of these kids are followers with no one to tell them right from wrong, but that's a whole other book.

"Please no sexually explicit comments towards the hosts. Treat them with the respect you would want someone to treat your mother, father, sister, brother, what have you."

There are two hosts on this program. AJ is a tall Black man, slim build with hair that is braided in rows in the front then from the middle are long dreads that fall to the small of his back. Free is a diminutive young woman with a strawberry blond curly afro and a voluptuous figure. She also has an easy smile. They both seem like happy people. Then again recording live in front of millions of viewers worldwide I guess you have to smile a lot even if you don't want to.

"Alright, I need two lines."

With that announcement kids that were sitting in various parts of the room jump up and rush to form disoriented lines. The man walks out of the room followed by the kids and me. We make the trek up two flights of stairs through a door. There is a main lobby area that leads to an open door, outside of which stands another person with a white T-shirt.

Upon entering the door the temperature drops a few degrees. To the left is a small stage with a coffee table in the middle and two small couches. As I move forward I see the main set of the show. There are

elaborate cameras set up everywhere.
One particular camera turned directly
at the incoming crowd is the
teleprompter. This camera will roll the
words that AJ and Free will speak
during the show.

   To the right and left of me are
bleachers that house the daily studio
audience. On the left side of the set
is a huge couch with multi-colored
pillow cushions spread across it.
Behind the couch is a wall with three
smalls screens imbedded into it.

   I scan to my right and see curtains
made of shingles. Several people from
the show's staff are going back and
forth through this curtain so I assume
it leads to the backstage area. Looking
further to my right I see the stage.
There are small speakers surrounding
the head of the stage. Two turntables
are set up at the back. I was less than
an hour away from taking my place
there.

   I started to get a bit nervous which
is customary before a big performance.
I searched the studio audience for Illa
Danz. I thought about how he destroyed
the previous "champion" to the point he
started looking at the DJ as if he

would start the record over. It was comical last week, but could that happen to me this week?

I started to think about a lot of things. This was gonna be on national TV. I couldn't embarrass myself. I told all my friends and family that I was going to be on this show. Family as far away as Jamaica would be watching me via satellite.

I gazed at the area next to the stage where two dozen replica platinum and gold covered albums were suspended along the wall. I was led to my seat at the top row of the right bleachers. I was staring directly at the stage where I would perform and I would do so for the next 50 minutes or so. Oh, the agony of it all.

AJ was the first host to make an appearance on stage from behind the curtain. This was customary for the hosts to appear on stage to go over any last minute issues. Sometimes they would talk to the audience. Although the show boasted that it was live, it was far from it because there were too many mistakes being made while reading the teleprompter.

There can be no do-overs on live television so to avoid the embarrassment the powers that be decided to pre-tape the shows. As Free made her way out to the set she received wild applause. The show was barely six months old, but Free had made an impact with her personable interviewing style, fashion sense (the hair, clothes and shoes), and her body was a hit with the guys.

The lady that gave me the opportunity to be here was the audience coordinator Annette. She was dressed in a red shirt and khakis. Her job was to make sure the studio audience was seated properly. Another young guy in the same attire stood in front of the bleachers where I was seated. I believe he was the assistant coordinator slash hype man.

"Come on, clap it up," he would say while frantically waving his hand in an upward motion that signaled the audience to make some noise.

He was in charge of getting the audience to applaud at the beginning of the show, in and out of commercial breaks, and when a celebrity guest said something deemed worthy of praise. At this particular moment the show was officially beginning and our collective applause would coincide with the opening theme music of the show.

The other cameras in the studio were on wheels and were being moved across the front of the bleachers panning the audience before the camera with the teleprompter went on to show AJ and Free.

"You are witnessing the livest audience on television," begins Free. "I am Free."

"And I'm AJ".

"It's Friday and you know what that means," continued Free.

"That's right. It's Freestyle Friday," said AJ.

They bounced off of one another effortlessly, each picking up the other.

"The reigning champion Illa Danz is back to go for his second win in a row. He will be taking on a new challenger. Can't wait for that," Free said.

Damn, Free. No name recognition to start the show? I was still anonymous

and, as I would see later, not expected
to do much of anything against the
current champ.

Coming up to the commercial break
that would precede my segment I got
more nervous. Suddenly the studio
audience is instructed to clap. As I
put my hands together with the rest of
the audience, I have my eyes on
Annette. She is wearing a black headset
with an attached microphone. She
already knew where I was in the crowd
because, naturally, she seated me.
Suddenly she turned to me:

"MBF!"

I jump up immediately upon hearing
my pseudonym. It felt like all eyes
were on me as I made my descent down
the bleachers. I was overcome by a huge
rush of nervous energy as I stepped
past a sea of audience members.

"We're going to come back from
commercial break, play a video, and
while the video is playing you will
take the stage," instructed Annette. A
huge roar comes up from the crowd as
another staffer with headphones runs to
each side of the room frantically
waving his hands to illicit noise. I

kept my eyes on the stage. There are three movie director style folding chairs placed in a horizontal row slightly in front of the turntables set.

"In a few minutes we're going to have our Freestyle Friday battle," says Free. She is looking very colorful in a red knit sweater and tight, hip-hugging blue jeans.

"That's right, the returning champ Illa Danz will go for his second straight win against a new challenger," says AJ.

These two fresh faces were new to the public eye, hired by BET Networks to be the face of their own version of a video countdown show that aired on the rival MTV network. The chemistry between AJ and Free was usually heightened by the sexual tension which, wholly initiated by AJ, on the surface appears to be one-sided.

"But first here's the latest video from Ginuwine," says Free.

And with that the video for "There It Is" by Ginuwine appeared on the big screen in the studio. I will never forget that song. The house DJ for the week appeared from backstage and took his place behind the turntables set. I stepped up onto the stage and took my place to the right of the turntables. I was given a microphone and a huge chain link with a sign that read "Challenger" was placed around my neck.

When they gave me the microphone it finally hit me. As I looked down at the shiny chrome, I immediately came to the realization that in a few minutes I was going to be broadcast in millions of homes around the world.

The champ Illa Danz appeared from the opposite end of the bleachers I was sitting in. It was like he was strategically kept out of sight to give the effect of some sort of grand entrance, nice if you're a five-time champ totally unnecessary for a one-week winner.

Danz looked the part of confident incumbent. He rocked a gray hooded sweater with a baseball cap turned backwards, black jeans and boots. He was given his microphone and the chain link sign that hung from his neck read "Champion".

I started to move from side to side. Others bite their nails when they're nervous, I rock from left to right. The stage was a little warmer than the rest of the studio because of all the lights shining. The added heat did not help.

I kept wiping the palms of my hands on my sweater almost subconsciously until I realized they were soaking wet from anxiety. It felt like I had Patrick Ewing's pre-game sweat glands.

I looked out into the crowd and all eyes were on me. It was like when AJ started explaining the rules of the contest he was actually reading my last rites. The entire studio was eerily silent. You could hear a rat piss on cotton. If I looked hard enough I could have sworn I saw pity in the eyes of some of the girls in the crowd. If I didn't know any better it would seem like I was getting blindfolded and ready to be put in front of a firing squad.

The judges began to make their way onto the stage. Renowned actor Morris Chestnut, of *Boyz N' Da Hood* and *The Best Man* fame along with other notable films is the prohibitive favorite amongst the young ladies. As he takes his seat, Chestnut is greeted by catcalls and a smattering of applause. He acknowledges the show of affection with his trademark smile and takes his seat to the far end of the stage.

Recording artist Jahiem is the second judge to appear on stage. Jahiem was a relatively new artist at this time, his single *"Just in Case"* and subsequent debut album made him a star. He took his seat next to Morris Chestnut as rap artist Fat Joe made his way onto the stage. The third and final judge, Joe is a rap veteran who released a number of albums dating back to his 1993 debut.

Free took her place to the right of the judges. By now my grandfather clock movements did not go unnoticed by the crowd as some began to whisper amongst themselves. The majority of the building did not give me a lit match's chance in Alaska to win this battle.

I was rocking to an imaginary beat by now, or so I made it seem. I showed no emotion so it was hard for the crowd to read me I guess. While I was confident I would be able to compete, the stoicism of the studio audience brought about a sliver of doubt and fear of embarrassing myself on national television that was in direct competition with the desire to prove my doubters wrong.

Deep down in my gut the outcome was never really in question. This was the biggest stage I had ever graced to this point and if I wanted a serious career in Hip Hop music, I would have to seize this opportunity to show the world what I could do. Eminem would make a song about this type of scenario called "Lose Yourself" in 2002. But I was not thinking about Eminem at the moment.

"Ten seconds," yelled a staffer.

I felt a sharp nervous sensation in my stomach as the chorus to Ginuwine's song reverberated through the studio. The audience is implored to cheer as the video dissolves into a live shot of the stage and its occupants.

"That was 'There It Is' by Ginuwine, number 4 on the countdown today," says Free. "Now it's time for this week's edition of Freestyle Friday and if you have been watching you know our returning champ. Say what's up to the people."

"What's going on? It's Illa Danz representing Jersey," Danz intones in a gruff voice.

"Okay and today we have a new challenger. What's your name, family?" AJ asks.

"I go by the name of MBF from East Flatbush, Brooklyn".

Still calm and collected as I spoke the area of my stomping grounds the crowd cheered. I continued to sway from side to side as Free introduced the judges. AJ went over the rules of the competition for the viewers watching around the world:

"There is no cursing, no sexually explicit material..."

After AJ completed the rules, he instructed us to touch microphones. The DJ dropped the beat. Neither myself or Danz knew what the track would be, but as the first chords of "Let Me Blow Your Mind" by Eve featuring Gwen Stefani started to play I jumped in as soon as the baseline and the drum kicked in.

"I smash amateurs...," I rhymed. My whole voice changed up, my countenance transformed from expressionless bopper to MC with a purpose. I only had half a bar to catch the beginning of the beat on time if I wanted to start at that moment. Otherwise I would have to wait for the beat to roll around after four bars which would have been a disaster.

It had to be fate that the DJ decided to choose that instrumental at that time. It was perfect. I moved fluidly turning my attention back and forth from Danz to the crowd. It was like I was performing an intimate concert. Every line had a play on words that got a response from the audience. It was the kind of reaction that arises out of shock.

I turned to Jahiem and extended my hand in his direction: "flow mean and get 'Ghetto Love' like Jahiem." "OOOOOOOhhhhh," roared the crowd.

"Ghetto Love" was the name of Jahiem's debut album that featured the aforementioned 'Just in Case' single. Jahiem appreciated the shout throwing up the peace sign in my direction.

I was on a roll. I was moving fluidly in my imaginary box. I felt like a ballroom dancer with little footprints spread out on the floor in a two-step sequence. I took two steps toward Danz careful not to break the imaginary line between us, I took two steps backwards, turned my left foot towards the stage with my right following in one motion where I was facing the crowd, rocking to the beat and rattling off wordplay:

"rhymes I sling out/ your girl see me whip her t(it)s out…"

The place exploded. It was not only the sheer disrespect of what I said that got everyone going, but that I was able to censor myself – remember there was no cursing – that got such a strong reaction. It was a risky move because I could have gotten disqualified, but I had to lay it all out there. If I was going to lose to Illa Danz he would catch every bullet I had in my arsenal.

I didn't know Danz's girl or if he had a girl for that matter. In a battle there is no holds barred. Sure the best material comes from thorough research of an opponent or if he or she is misguided enough to wear something crazy that can be picked apart, but I only had 30 seconds and saying his significant other would strip when she saw me was just the low blow I needed to get some points with the people. It also showed I had confidence and a slight arrogance about me they could not see three minutes earlier as I sweated under the hot stage lights waiting for the battle to start.

Make no mistake about it the studio audience is the fourth judge. Their reaction one way or another can sway the opinion of the people sitting in the chair on stage. It was the performer in me that told me I had to play to the crowd and get them involved. It told them I was here to win so naturally I threw one last salvo in my final two bars as the DJ put a backspin on the record to let me know my time was up:

"Just give me 90 seconds for fun," I spit as I looked at the DJ. As I turned back to Danz I continued "and I'll smoke you so many times got the crowd giving me Nicorette gum."

A thunderous applause rose from the crowd. I definitely felt the love from the room and immediately put my two arms in the air and raised the roof a few times as I paced the stage. My back was to the crowd at this point, but a review of footage of this battle showed that a few audience members put their hands up in response to my gesture.

I was proud of myself. I made it through the 30 seconds unscathed and I think I successfully opened some eyes with my performance. There was still a buzz in the studio. I look into the crowd to see what is happening and I'm immediately met with staring eyes. I find Annette in the audience and she is looking at me in amazement clapping along with the rest of the audience. On the outside I react as if I have been here before, no smiles of self-satisfaction or outward patting myself on the back.

While I was pleased that I shattered the perception of me, my job was not done. I came here to win and the truth of the matter was Illa Danz still had 30 seconds to respond to my surprising outburst. I didn't know what to expect from him. I remember him destroying the champion a week ago.

The nervous pangs in my stomach returned. There was no beat on and I was not performing so all my nervous energy returned. It was like Superman turning back into Clark Kent or The

Incredible Hulk calming down and changing back into Bruce Banner. The audience was looking at me like I was naked except for some torn pants turned into shorts.

"Alright, settle down," Free implored. Free of all people probably knew what I was feeling at that moment. She was an artist herself. Upon later review of the footage of my 30 seconds she was getting a kick out of my rhymes along with Morris Chestnut.

That is all I wanted as an MC: to say things that made people jump up and down with excitement or make people want to rewind or ask the person next to them if he or she heard what I said.

"It is now time for the champion Illa Danz. You've got 30 seconds," explained Free.

I stole a quick glance at Danz and saw his eyes were looking down at the floor. He was just as shocked as the rest of the studio at what he just witnessed. His mind was working overtime. I knew he was going to come just as hard to try to retain his crown. I did not know what to expect I just hoped what I did was enough to win.

The music started up again and Danz did not jump on the beat drop as I did filling the first four bars of the track with filler "Yo, Yo…!": So far so good, I thought.

"Like Boyz N' Da Hood my flow is lethal…," began Danz. As I did with Jahiem, Danz went for the name drop of the movie to try to swing favor with Morris Chestnut. It was a calculated move, but it came too early in the rhyme, I thought. When I dropped Jahiem's album title I was already two bars in and building momentum off an opening punch line. I stole a quick look at Chestnut for his reaction and while he was smiling, he didn't seem impressed.

That would change shortly. Danz had his right hand closed for the entire segment. I thought nothing of it. Then it came: the line of the entire battle. Danz was pretty animated, his lines punctuated by a series of hand movements. I made it my duty to stand completely still and show no emotion during his entire time and I succeeded for the most part. I didn't want to give Danz an extra edge by looking like I was in awe of him in any way. He was spittin' just as hard and angry as he had been the previous week. He took a step toward me and cocked his right hand back and swung at my face:

"I'll run in your mouth and look I came out with a few teeth, too..."

The punch was imaginary, but it might as well have hit me square in the jaw. After finishing the line, Danz opened his right hand and tiny balled up pieces of white paper fell to the stage. These little balls were supposed to be my teeth.

The crowd erupted. Free jumped up and down with laughter next to Morris Chestnut whose closed mouth grin now expanded to a wide smile. On the exterior I appeared unmoved staring blankly at my competitor who was attacking me with great ferocity, fighting desperately to keep his spot as champion, but inside my eyes closed.

It was a great line no doubt about it and for a moment I thought that would be my undoing. I knew in a battle whoever was the champion had the psychological edge because he or she had been there before. It was my job as challenger to overcome this subconscious advantage.

It was like I was the prosecution in a court case with the burden of proof to sway the jury and Illa Danz put up a hell of a defense.

A lot of what Danz was saying after that was a blur to me. I just wanted to hear the record backspin. The longer Danz had a chance to rhyme the more I felt like he had a chance to take me out. I just kept thinking how quick my time on stage seemed to go by, but watching and waiting for Danz to finish seemed like time had stopped and I would keep getting hit with a barrage of similes and metaphors until I was finally pounded into submission.

It was the longest 30 seconds of my life.

Finally a backspin interrupts what felt like a 60 second verbal beating. The studio is buzzing again. In what would go down as one of the best battles in the young history of "Freestyle Friday" according to a BET staffer, the judges had a tough decision in front of them. I was glad to be a part of this moment. I would love to win, but if I don't…

I didn't want to think about it. I felt I was too good not to win at least one week. If I lost I would not only have to wear the stench of being a loser like a cheap suit, I would be faced with the prospect of fading away into obscurity. My 15 minutes of fame would be short by 14 and 30 seconds. I couldn't go out like that, but it was not up to me. It was all in the judges' hands now.

As Danz walked over to A.J. where I had already been standing I looked down at the front of the stage littered with those tiny paper balls and thought I could lose because of those dead trees. It was genius. I couldn't be mad at that.

"Alright," said Free still trying to contain her laughter. "That was our Freestyle Friday battle. Judges it's on you. Mr. Morris Chestnut."

My stomach was doing somersaults. I needed two out of the three judges to call my name to win. I was confident I had Jahiem's vote, but Fat Joe remained expressionless the entire battle. It was all on Morris Chestnut who pretty much had the same reaction to both of us.

"Hmm, it was real tough, man," Chestnut said. "Both guys were good." He then paused. I guess the movie star in him had to add to the suspense. I wanted to tell him 'this was not a movie Morris, spit it out.'

"I'm gonna have to go with the challenger."

I couldn't believe he picked me. My right hand immediately went up in his direction as a silent thank you. He nodded his head and gave me a peace sign in return. I was nodding my head still keeping my emotion concealed, but inside I was doing cartwheels. It was all on Jahiem.

"Man," he said shaking his head. "Woo."

"Okay?" Free chimed in agreement.

"I was digging my man right here," Jahiem said pointing to Illa Danz.

I was waiting for a 'but' at any moment. There had to be. Jahiem looked over in my direction.

"My man did shout me out though," he said smiling.

Then **he** went silent. What was it with the silence before making a decision with these guys? Were they trying to give me a heart attack?

After looking at both of us one last time, Jahiem finally pursed his lips to speak his decision.

"I'ma have to go wit my man right here."

He never specified who he was picking although I saw him pointing at me, at least that's what I wanted to see.

"The challenger?" asked Free.

"Yeah, the challenger."

Way to clarify, Free. I breathed a huge sigh of relief. I had received two out of two votes which made Fat Joe's pick irrelevant. I was glad because something told me Joe was going to pick against me. He was Fat Joe the Gangsta when he burst onto the scene in the early '90s and Illa Danz was spitting hardcore lyrics.

"It don't matter what I say now, do it?" asked Joe with a smile.

"Of course it does," said Free.

"I'm gonna go with the champion, man. He was spittin' that fire."

"There it is, one for the champion Illa Danz," said AJ.

Danz clapped it up appreciative of the vote. At least it wasn't a sweep. It didn't deserve to be.

Grandma's Boys

I think my grandma called home her
boys/ first my dad then my uncle Bois/
e - the nickname for my uncle Cliff/
who without warning suffered a stroke -

but why would God revoke his gift of
life/ and at the same time promote his
soul from pain and strife/

questions asked by us mere humans/ in
this game of life - we fall in love
with family to eventually lose them/

we on pins and needles when the
diseases and toxins/ make a strong man
feeble a superhero our equal/ we
feeling boxed in cuz we pleading for
relief when Jesus is screaming
"I am!"

See Grandma's boys are with Him - with
her/ so she's not alone/ that's all she

wanted those last years in the nursing
home –

crying to come home anywhere but
there/ everywhere those dear to her
resided/ but no one wanted her so He
provided

Rest amongst the clouds eternal life He
vowed/ healing from the sunlight
surround sound/ of angel music/ no
arthritis no sores none of that
abusive/

pain that felt domestic because it
lived with you 24-7/ still she felt a
void that made her question was this
heaven... She was missing her boys –

So she called them home – one in 2012
one in 2013 – cuz she left this Earth
in 2008/

four years enough time for her boy to
start a clean slate/ for her Boisy
to reach the gate/ never mind the
family making noise at his wake/

on her watch
it was their time
She couldn't wait – for her boys

"I'm Coming Home"

Those three words were the conclusion to a heartfelt essay published on the website of Sports Illustrated (SI.com) on July 11, 2014 by veteran journalist Lee Jenkins as told to him by NBA superstar LeBron James. Four years after LeBron broke the collective hearts of the city of Cleveland by announcing his decision to leave the Cavaliers for the Miami Heat, Akron, Ohio's favorite son reversed his course and told the world he was returning to the state of his humble beginnings.

Instantly all was "For6iven", as one hastily printed T-shirt proclaimed, and just like that Cleveland will once again be the center of the basketball universe. But why did the King leave in the first place? What pushed the best basketball player in the world to make the most polarizing choice in modern sports history? Rumors persist that

LeBron's mind was already made up as far back as 2008 when he, Dwyane Wade, and Chris Bosh were members of the United States Olympic basketball team.

Whether true or not there were many mitigating factors involved in pushing LeBron out of the proverbial door. In the humble opinion of this writer read on to see what I believe led to…

THE DECISION

*WHAT WAS LEBRON JAMES THINKING?**

* LEBRON JAMES, HIS FAMILY, FRIENDS, TEAMMATES, EX-TEAMMATES, FANS, DETRACTORS, CRITICS, OR MEDIA MEMBERS DID NOT CONTRIBUTE ANY INFORMATION TO THIS STORY.

"Okay, LeBron. The moment everyone has been waiting for…," uttered reporter Jim Gray in the understatement of the summer of 2010, possibly the year.

"What's your decision?" he continued.

"My decision…" He paused slightly. "Woo this is tough…"

At that moment, with just that slight hesitation to reveal his choice, I knew LeBron James was definitely leaving Cleveland. Was he going to my beloved New York Knicks? After all the broadcast of James' decision called, very imaginatively I might add, "The Decision" on where he would play basketball for the foreseeable future was taking place at a Boys and Girls club in nearby Connecticut, close to where the Knicks practice.

He had taken heat (no pun intended) for allegedly quitting on his team in the 2010 playoffs against the Boston Celtics. Still since coming into the league in 2003 with enough pressure to bust a million pipes, "The Chosen One" (one of those nicknames that naturally won't cause anyone to pay attention to you) lived up to and exceeded the hype from his very first NBA game in Sacramento.

He singlehandedly made the Cavaliers relevant again, something that had not happened since Michael Jordan put the final nail in the coffin of the Lenny Wilkens-era when he burned Gerald Wilkins - the self-described "Jordan stopper" - with "The Shot part II" in 1993.

LeBron led Cleveland to their first playoff win since 1992, took them to the NBA Finals without a legitimate supporting cast in 2007, and to the best record in the NBA in 2009 and 2010. The Cavs were upset by the Orlando Magic in the Eastern Conference Finals, a series remembered for LeBron's catch and shoot game winning three-pointer in Game 2 and the way he left the court without shaking the hands of the Magic players after the series clinching Game 6 defeat.

The series against Orlando exposed a flawed defense against the three-point shot. The Cavs had no answer for Magic forwards Hedo Turkoglu and Rashard Lewis - both taller than 6'8" LeBron - who blistered the front court with a 3 point barrage that brought them back to win Game 1 and set the tone for the series.

Cleveland had gone 66-16 during the '08-'09 NBA campaign and the only team that was thought to be a threat to the Cavs was the defending champion Boston Celtics, a veteran team anchored by three future Hall of Famers Kevin Garnett, Paul Pierce, and Ray Allen and dubbed "The Big Three" when they assembled just a year earlier.

The Celtics beat LeBron and the Cavs in the '08 Eastern Conference Semifinals in a spirited Game 7 showdown between James and Pierce that was shades of the classic Larry Bird-Dominique Wilkins Game 7 duel of 1988. James outscored Pierce 45-41, but the Celtics bench (namely P.J. Brown) made the key plays down the stretch to thwart a Conference Finals rematch between LeBron and the Detroit Pistons.

With Orlando disposing of Boston in seven games, the road to the Finals and a matchup with the Lakers was practically set in stone. All the "experts" had the Cavaliers winning the series. Why wouldn't they? They were all witnesses (pun intended) to how LeBron took over that 2007 playoff game against the Pistons, how he pushed the Celtics to the brink in 2008, and how he dominated the Pistons and Hawks in consecutive four-game sweeps to start the '09 playoffs in which he led the team in scoring in all eight games and assists in six of the eight.

After jumping out to two first quarter double-digit leads at home against Orlando, that LeBron's miracle three was needed to save the Cavs from going down 0-2 should have been an ominous sign. I mean if I scored 49 points and dished off 8 assists and my team still blew a double digit halftime lead to lose by one point, I would be pissed. Faced with that prospect in Game 2 and still have the stones to take, and hit, the winning three with a 6'10" Lewis flying past you? That's clutch. That is a man with a will to win.

Yet two consecutive 40-plus point scoring efforts in Games 3 and 4 yielded losses and a 3-1 deficit. 41 points and 9 assists in Game 3 and lose by 10? 44 points 12 rebounds and 7 assists just to lose in overtime after blowing another halftime lead? You have to start thinking where's the help. It's only natural.

LeBron took matters into his own hands throwing up 37-14-12 on an unsuspecting Magic squad to save his season. He led the team to 66 wins, the best record in the entire league. No Cleveland team had won that many games ever in franchise history. This wasn't the Celtics. Surely his run was not going to be stopped by Dwight Howard and two players who were role players on their former teams (Turkoglu in

Sacramento, Lewis in Seattle respectively).

Well, the Magic scored 58 first half points with a superior inside-outside attack that was a microcosm of the entire series. LeBron could only guard one person. He could only score so many points. With Dwight Howard scoring 40 points and pulling down 14 rebounds at center there was no way to guard him one-on-one. Double team Howard and Turkoglu and Lewis made you pay.

Down by 18 points at halftime the Cavaliers lost by 13. LeBron quickly made his way off the court only looking back a few times. Surely he was humiliated. Mo Williams, brought in to take some of the offensive pressure off of James, did none of that in the Orlando series. Williams, who emerged as a scoring threat while a member of the Milwaukee Bucks, was brought in by general manager Danny Ferry for his outside shooting prowess.

Williams paid dividends during the regular season making the All-Star team in 2009. However during the playoffs his shot was inconsistent. The offensive load LeBron carried for the Cavs can be compared to Michael

Jordan's early years in Chicago save for the fact James was very adept at passing the ball.

Now I played basketball with people that were better than me offensively and I remember how they reacted the, ahem, rare times I missed a shot after being setup with a great pass. I can only imagine the agony LeBron felt losing a series to Orlando that they probably should have won in five games.

Roundly criticized for the unsportsmanlike manner in which he left the court after the Game 6 defeat, James told the press that he hated to lose. He wasn't going to shake hands with a team that beat him because he was that much of a competitor.

That logic didn't fly in a sport that preaches sportsmanship and teamwork. Especially being one of the superstars chosen (no pun intended) to be the face of the NBA. LeBron looked like a sore loser that season, his feelings exacerbated by the fact that Orlando went on to go out without a fight against the Los Angeles Lakers in the Finals.

In a return to the NBA Finals, James had to be thinking he would not have gotten swept again, first of all, and that the Kobe-LeBron matchup was what everyone wanted to see and he failed to deliver on his part of the bargain. But it wasn't for lack of trying.

Could it have been possible that he had his eye out the door of Cleveland at this time? The 2009-2010 season would be his last under his current contract. Even though it took Jordan seven seasons to win his first championship, in this what-have-you-done-for-me-lately 21st century league, six years was too long.

One of two things could have been going through LeBron's head: I can come out guns blazing in my final year and go all out to give Cleveland its first title and stamp my place as the most legendary figure in Cleveland sports history or if I don't get the job done would I ever win in Cleveland? My bet is he believed he could do the former.

Nike had gotten ahead of itself during the season creating puppets of LeBron and Kobe in anticipation of a Finals matchup that did not materialize.

The puppets were back for a second year in 2010 and defending champion Kobe was poking fun at LeBron in the commercials. James seemed poised to get his team over the hump. He might not have gone to management directly, but they knew they had to surround him with a better supporting cast if they wanted a snowball's chance at The North Pole of keeping him after the season.

Aging superstar Shaquille O'Neal was brought in to be a wall in the middle, Antawn Jamison, an All-Star forward, was a versatile big who could shoot the 3-point shot, and Mo Williams, the point guard who flamed out against Orlando was back to try to redeem himself.

The following year LeBron was a beast in the 2010 season, winning his second straight MVP award, and in the playoffs, steamrolling the upstart Chicago Bulls in the first round and playing the Celtics tough in taking a convincing 2-1 series lead - behind a 38-point effort from James - handing the Celtics their worst home loss (29 points) in their storied playoff history.

The Cavs were favored to win the series and set up the dream matchup with Kobe Bryant and the Lakers.

In Game 4 James was not the same player he was in the previous 7 postseason games. His passes, usually pinpoint, were sloppy and misguided. He was turning the ball over. Rajon Rondo, an assist machine, torched the Cavs for a triple-double 29-18-13 (points-rebounds-assists) that felt like no one was guarding him at the point guard position.

To the naked eye LeBron looked lost, a shell of himself. It was almost like he did not want to be on the court. I was dumbfounded, but I didn't think anything of it. He had a 2-1 series lead and the Celtics had the Big 3 and Rondo. They were not going to be as easy as the Bulls.

In Game 5 it was more of the same. The Cavaliers were on their home floor. This is the advantage they fought the entire season to have. Yet after winning the first quarter 23-20, the Cavs gave up 30 points in the second and third quarters and 40 in the fourth en route to an embarrassing 120-88 defeat.

LeBron wasn't even the leading scorer for Cleveland. It was the 38 year-old O'Neal who led the way with 21 points. This wasn't 2001. O'Neal was far removed from his heyday with the Los Angeles Lakers yet here he was leading the scoring "attack".

That LeBron didn't break the 20 point barrier was even more glaring. This wasn't the same guy that had the fire in his belly during the aforementioned performances of playoffs past. This wasn't the same man who let out a primal yell after throwing down a right handed tomahawk dunk as he flew across the lane in the first round against the Bulls. Number 23 had something on his mind, but fans of the Cavaliers did not want to hear it. They accused LeBron of quitting, a slap in the face to any professional athlete.

The conspiracy theorist in me assumed LeBron saw how Rondo carved up Mo Williams in Game 4 and became disillusioned with his team. Perhaps he had a feeling of déjà vu from the Conference Finals against Orlando the year before when his team snatched defeat from the jaws of victory despite his best efforts.

Maybe the realization hit LeBron as he looked around that he had nobody that played point guard like Rondo, no one that shot the ball like Ray Allen. That 38 year-old Shaquille O'Neal wasn't enough to stop K.G., let alone Dwight Howard.

The reality of the situation was this: expectations for Cleveland skyrocketed when LeBron put a mediocre team on his back all the way to the Finals in 2007. The pressure was on Danny Ferry to surround James with a decent supporting cast so he could accomplish the unthinkable: bringing an NBA title, check that, a title in any sport to the Buckeye state.

To his credit Ferry revamped the roster around James every subsequent season trying to find the right mix including acquiring O'Neal and Jamison to counter the size of Dwight Howard, still this time they couldn't stop the smallest guy on the court.

2010 was an all or nothing year for Cleveland. The talk the entire season was whether or not winning a title would validate LeBron bolting to another team in free agency. He could always say he gave Cleveland a championship and now it was on to his next challenge. Or he could bask in the glow of doing what no professional sports figure had done and sign on to spend his entire career with the Cavs while posing for the inevitable statue the city and state would erect in his honor.

That was all a moot point. The team he led onto the Quicken Loans Arena floor for Game 5 of the 2010 Eastern Conference semifinals lost by 32 points. And for the second game in a row he played with no passion. I had never seen anything like it.

What was wrong with LeBron?

Despite posting the quietest triple-double ever by a superstar in a playoff game, LeBron and the Cavs bowed out in Game 6 to Boston. James quickly stripped off his Cleveland jersey before he left the court and entered the tunnel. Perhaps he knew then it was his last game as a member of the Cavaliers.

Still the season-ending 3-game losing streak left many scratching their heads. Soon the ugliest of rumors would surface. Gloria James, LeBron's mother and biggest supporter, was allegedly sleeping with one of her son's teammates.

Gloria was a visible presence at numerous Cleveland home games vociferously cheering on her only child. Yet allegations suggested she was a bigger fan of someone else: Delonte West. West was a shooting guard that gave the team life off the bench with his outside shooting. As the alleged story goes, West was bedding James' mom in hotels and James accidentally walked in on them in action when he went to check on her at one particular venue.

Nasty.

James never addressed these rumors, but another teammate Wally Szcerbiak all but confirmed he had heard about the affair actually taking place. Websites like Deadspin.com posted e-mails citing sources within the Cleveland "Cavaliers front office" stating that Delonte West had been "hooking up with Gloria James for some time now. Somehow I guess LeBron found out before game four and it has destroyed the teams chemistry and divided the team…" Source:

http://deadspin.com/5544653/anatomy-of-
a-rumor-how-the-gloria-james-delonte-
west-sex-story-went-viral

Wow.

The fact that LeBron even showed up
to play (in the physical form, anyway)
in those games is a testament to his
professionalism. Assuming this is true,
beyond the sheer embarrassment of not
knowing this was happening, the fact
that it is your mother - a woman old
enough to be the mother of most of your
teammates - that she would put herself
in that position, that your teammates
allegedly knew this was going on and
none of them bothered to tell you about
it, how could he trust these guys ever
again?

Forget about on a basketball court,
you have to have some kind of
relationship off the court with your
teammates to succeed. There has to be
some sort of affection for the people
you are going to battle with. You see
pictures of the Chicago Bulls of the
'90s playing cards on the plane in
Sports Illustrated, the Showtime Lakers
sitting in a roundtable on NBATV
gushing about how they genuinely loved
each other and you think there had to

be some sort of camaraderie between LeBron and somebody on the squad.

Yet, if this indiscretion was true, he had to be thinking 'who else knew about this?' and 'How could y'all do this to me?'

Something happened that had James distracted over those last three games of the Boston series and "Gloria-gate" was being reported in too many places for it to be untrue in my opinion.

Again, while this alleged incident was never proven to be true in any factual report, LeBron never disputed the rumor in public. His mom never came out and defended her name. If this is just an ugly, hurtful allegation why not come out and vehemently deny it and defend the honor of your mother? If he did it wasn't definitive enough.

I can't front, I would feel betrayed by West definitely and by those in the locker room who knew about it and chose to say nothing. LeBron is the star of the team. Maybe those that knew were in shock and did not want to hurt him, but in effect did the complete opposite. Not speaking up would lead James to believe his team never cared about him as a person just what he could do on a basketball court to make them look better.

What a way to go into the summer of 2010. The speculation began after LeBron refused to extend his contract letting it be known that he would test free agency and weigh his options. He said as much on Larry King Live and other media outlets that inquired about his intentions.

All that drama led to a makeshift stage in the Boys and Girls club in Connecticut.

Everyone waited for July 1st, the official start of the free agency period. There were other stars who were free agents-to-be. Phoenix Suns forward Amare Stoudamire, Atlanta Hawks guard Joe Johnson, Utah Jazz forward Carlos Boozer, Toronto Raptors forward Chris Bosh, Miami Heat guard Dwyane Wade. Every single one of these guys were All-Stars. Still no star was bigger than LeBron. Analysts were predicting which combination of players would go where… as it pertained to a package attractive enough to lure LeBron.

It looked like no one was going to make a move until LeBron made his decision. In New York I heard all kinds of combinations. The Knicks had spent three years -some would argue trashing seasons - gutting their roster to give themselves enough cap room to sign LeBron and another big free agent. It was a risk for a team that was mired in a rut of mediocrity caused by irresponsible spending and overblown contracts to sub-par players throughout the first decade of the 21st century, but with a superior basketball mind in Donnie Walsh at the helm the risk would be worth the reward. Many different combinations were being thrown around: Joe Johnson and LeBron, Bosh and LeBron. Oh to dream.

This was to be the biggest event of the year. There were people billing LeBron as the biggest free agent in the history of sports. I think that was kind of stretching it, but definitely the biggest free agent of the era was about to decide where to play basketball for the next four to six years.

He had no less than five teams publicly courting him - the Cleveland Cavaliers, the aforementioned Knicks,

New Jersey (soon-to-be Brooklyn) Nets, Chicago Bulls, Los Angeles Clippers and Miami Heat - playing on his affections, hoping to convince him that their franchise is capable of winning for. Not to mention the entire free agent crop had stopped everything depending on where LeBron was going.

James was very careful not to tip his hand one way or the other during the roughly six weeks between the end of his season and the night of July 8, 2010. He and his team of advisors (he is managed by his best friend Maverick Carter) met with the aforementioned teams in Cleveland, giving hope to the Cavaliers faithful that since LeBron did not take part in the city-by-city tour, that would have no doubt tried to sweep him off his feet with elaborate presentations and trips to different landmarks, his first choice would be to stay in the city that raised him.

Still there the prognosticators were out in full force. Fans were glued to ESPN insiders like Stephen A. Smith and Chris Broussard for any clues to who was a frontrunner in the LeBron James sweepstakes. It seemed like every day it was a different team. One team everyone definitely crossed off the list was the Los Angeles Clippers.

No disrespect to the "other" team from Los Angeles, a league wide laughingstock for many years since Danny Manning left town, the Clippers were getting a healthy Blake Griffin back (Griffin missed his entire rookie season with a broken kneecap), they had a center in Chris Kaman that could score, guard Eric Gordon and Baron Davis who, when interested, was still one of the best point guards in the NBA.

The Clippers were very inviting, except for the fact that they play in the same city as Kobe Bryant and the Lakers. LeBron was already getting abused by Kobe as a puppet, did he really want to play second fiddle to him in real life? He was already the face of a franchise that has long been haunted by the specter of Michael Jeffrey Jordan, I doubt he would want to be the face of another team with a less than stellar history.

Could it be the Knicks? He has gone on record as saying the Yankees are his favorite team. He even wore a New York Yankees cap in Cleveland when they played the Indians. He has played many of his best games at Madison Square Garden (but, then again who hasn't?). The Knicks had just signed All-Star power forward Amar'e Stoudamire away from the Phoenix Suns in a last second attempt to sway King James.

The case could be made for the Nets, who were the first to present to James. They wouldn't be moving to Brooklyn for a couple of years but Jay-Z was a close personal friend. I mean, if this wasn't a legal visit in the eyes of the NBA it would be considered tampering, close personal friend. James appeared on magazine covers with Jay-Z at the time surrounded by the roster of Roc-a-Fella Records. A billionaire owner looking to make a splash in Mikhail Prokorov making no secret of the fact that money was not an option. Seemed like a slam dunk right?

The Chicago Bulls had Derrick Rose, an otherworldly point guard, a scrappy center in Joakim Noah and enough cash to add another maximum contract player along with James. There was talk that Dwyane Wade would leave Miami and go play for his native hometown in Chicago. Rumors even swirled that Chris Bosh would be the second player headed to Chicago with LeBron. If Chicago could pull that off just hand over the Larry O'Brien trophy to the Windy City for another six years.

Those dreams would be wishful thinking as the Bulls would sign LeBron's former teammate Carlos Boozer while Bosh agreed to sign with Miami. Both of those big men were significant upgrades from what LeBron was working with on the front line in Cleveland. Would these moves be enough to pull James away from the Cavaliers?

Talk about pressure. This man has stood up to the Mack truck of expectations levied upon him since he was a pre-teen and faced it head-on and won. However this decision had to be the most nerve-racking, emotional, life-changing choices he ever had to make.

Forget about the money, just think about how the fans of Cleveland would react if he decided to leave for another team. This is the city in a state he was born and raised in, won high school championships, hoisted a 50 foot poster on the side of the arena in his likeness with the slogan from the shoe and apparel company that signed him to a $90 million contract before he played an NBA game. The city that he brought as close to an NBA championship than they have ever been even when the legendary Lenny Wilkens coached the team, the city that would most likely change the name of a major landmark to LeBron's name once he chooses to retire.

Then think about if he did decide to play for another NBA team the fact that he would singlehandedly swing the balance of power in the entire league.

No sweat.

"Do you have any doubts about your decision?" asked Gray.

"No. I don't have any doubts at all," LeBron would say with a face as emotionless as a stone statue.

"Would you like to sleep on it a little longer?" Gray would inquire.

Damn, Jim. If I didn't know any better it sounded like Gray was one of the "handful" of people that already knew LeBron's decision and was trying to talk him out of it.

It was time for the world to know LeBron's decision a little over five minutes into the start of the interview.

"The answer to the question everybody wants to know, LeBron what's your decision?"

That noise you hear is the city of Cleveland holding their collective breath. I'm sure at that moment you could hear a pin drop everywhere. To that end James had accomplished what he wanted to do. All eyes were on him. The biggest free agent in NBA history was about to bring the biggest recruiting session ever for a non-college player to an end.

Leave it to LeBron to answer the question and coin a phrase that would be jacked, stolen, spun, regurgitated, flipped, and abused relentlessly to describe a person moving on to a new endeavor:

"I'm gon' take my talents to South Beach and join the Miami Heat".

At that moment you could hear someone in the room clap before finally containing their excitement in a room that remained completely silent.

Consider that LeBron mentioned he was going to an **area** of Miami before stating the team name and you start to believe that Freudian slip may have been a deciding factor for he and his team of advisors.

Don't worry, LeBron I love South Beach too.

LeBron ironically praised his mother as the person who made him believe he was making the right decision stating he had a conversation with his mom that morning. This shows regardless of all that may have happened, the rumors, the perceived scandal, family always comes first.

Fans in Cleveland were devastated to say the least. LeBron jerseys were burned in the streets of Cleveland. A live feed of which was shown to James as he sat on the makeshift stage in the gymnasium across from Jim Gray. Clearly not expecting this reaction from his now former fan base, LeBron was clearly flustered.

Would they have called him a quitter if he had re-signed with the team? Well, duh… of course not. This was like the fine girl/boy dumping you via text message times one hundred. LeBron was slammed for the way he executed his departure from Cleveland via a televised interview. Scrutinized for not having the decency to let the Cleveland organization know he was leaving before going live on-air at ESPN.

Cleveland had no back-up plan for life without LeBron. Call it arrogance or stupidity on the part of owner Dan Gilbert, it was definitely bad business. LeBron ultimately decided what was best for his well-being and Gilbert was left with a gaping hole at small forward.

Shock soon gave way to seething anger as Gilbert soon went on a maniacal rant addressing the fans of Cleveland culminating with a bold prediction which stated his Cavaliers, who just lost the best player in the league, would win a championship before LeBron would in Miami. The owner was clearly emotional and reacted like a jilted lover.

If LeBron had any lingering doubts about his decision, Gilbert's tirade served as validation. LeBron's decline in popularity began there. Then the aforementioned pep rally served as the proverbial dagger.

LeBron's heart was certainly in the right place. He wanted to raise money for the Boys and Girls club where "The Decision" was being filmed. He knew anticipation of where he was going to play basketball would have everyone hanging on his every word. Why not help underprivileged kids?

And so it was on the eighth day of July 2010. The landscape of the NBA changed in a matter of minutes. The balance of power shifting like the scales of justice.

Conversely, the people of Miami were overjoyed to have one superstar and another All-star join the Mayor of Wade County. So happy were the people in the southern part of The Sunshine State that they celebrated their newest acquisitions the only way they knew how: party.

Not even 48 hours after LeBron's decision came down, a pep rally was scheduled to be held in honor of the newly christened "Big 3" inside American Airlines Arena.

The histrionics of the rally, the pomp and circumstance seemed as if LeBron, albeit unwillingly, was rubbing every team that he didn't pick and their fan base's nose in his decision. To that point he carried himself like a humble superstar, a willing teammate, a person who cared more about making others better than his own success. He most likely still was that guy inside, it just was not coming across in the raw emotion of the moment. Remember Chris Bosh left his former team in Toronto holding the bag as well. But who cared about Chris Bosh, right?

As he was lifted onto the stage, the newly christened number "6" emblazoned (after giving up the number 23 he claimed to preserve his idol Michael Jordan's legacy) on his back, his new teammates Bosh and Wade to his left, surely LeBron was filled with nerves. How would the new fan base receive him? Just the shock of actually wearing another jersey, that he was really in Miami, it all had to hit him at that moment.

As all three men turned around at the same time to meet the adoring crowd, Bosh immediately let out a primal yell of "Let's Go", Wade smiled from ear to ear and clapped like a man that has been here before, satisfied at the work he had done that may have just secured a few more championship trophies for his mantle. LeBron looked around seemingly unsure of what to do. This was a new place. Miami is always a great place to visit, but now he would have to make it home. Home had always been Ohio, whether it was Akron or Cleveland.

There had to be a moment where he wondered again if he made the right decision. He was now one-third of a so-called super team that was already placed in the NBA Finals before the ink was dry on their contracts, yet all he could muster was an awkward repeated head nod to a beat maybe only he could hear.

When it was time for the "interview" he seemed ready to play, not so much comfortable. Once he all but guaranteed the Heat would win "not 2, not 3, not 4, not 5, not 6, not 7…" titles, and that once the games start it would be "easy", it was pretty much "what did the five fingers say to the face…SLAP (a reference to comedian Dave Chappelle's classic imitation of music legend Rick James) in the face of the rest of the league.

The more James spoke it seemed the more excited he became about his new team, but the choice of words, man. He was sounding like a kid with a new toy that no one else had. Like Eddie Murphy's ice cream kid ("I got some ice cream and you can't have none…") from *Delirious*. And if you are on the other side of such outward display of braggadocio, it is normal to be a little turned off, upset even. We are human.

LeBron is human. So I was probably one of the very few that did not kill him for all the predictions and boastful talk. The man just made a life-altering decision to uproot his family for the chance to advance his career, to make sure when he leaves the game of basketball he is mentioned in the same breath as his idol Jordan, Magic Johnson, and others. If he felt pressure before, this move to Miami and the aftermath just busted a few million pipes.

What was he going to say? That he was going to lose? He just got finished doing that in two straight seasons where he was expected to win. Maybe he felt he had to openly claim victory now. That he had to change his mindset, speak it into existence. He had no excuses now. Bosh and Wade were ten times better than anybody Danny Ferry was able to sign to play next to him. The spurned fans would have to get over it.

And they would. But LeBron probably did not expect it would take as long as it would.

After the pyrotechnics flared out at American Airlines Arena, the criticism continued. The Miami Heat were suddenly the image of everything wrong with the NBA. There was talk that since LeBron and Wade were such great friends they planned to be free agents at the same time so they could team up as far back as the 2008 Olympics.

NBA luminaries came out of the woodwork with opinions about this new super team in South Beach. Michael Jordan shared that he would have never left Chicago and join Magic Johnson on the Lakers or Larry Bird on the Celtics. That the challenge was to beat the best to be the best. The loquacious

Charles Barkley echoed those sentiments, no surprise there.

The response from Wade, LeBron and Bosh was that those great Lakers, Celtics, and Bulls teams all had three great players. Bird had McHale and Parrish, Jordan had Pippen and Horace Grant, and Magic had Kareem and Worthy.

True indeed, but those Big 3's were a product of the draft and timely trades that took place before the respective championship runs began. Jordan, and Grant were drafted by Chicago and Pippen was acquired in a draft day trade with Seattle in 1987, four years before the first championship. Kareem was traded to the Lakers before Magic was drafted by the team and Worthy was drafted by the team and fit right in. Larry Bird and McHale were drafted by Boston while Parrish was traded to the team. None of those threesomes were all established stars when they came together.

LeBron, Wade, and Bosh were manufactured. Surely it can't be legal for them to just decide to sign with the same team. That's cheating, right? To say many people that were not fans of the Miami Heat felt this way would be an understatement. It was legal. Heat president Pat Riley made it happen. He cleared cap space just like the five other teams in line for LeBron's services. Who knows what happened. Maybe at the time Riley threw his six championship rings on a table and said to James "you want one of these"? Sometimes it is that simple.

These are certainly different times in the NBA. There was a time when rivalries really existed in the league. Players hated each other's guts. When the word rivalry is mentioned in any sport let alone basketball the Boston and New York teams come to mind. Whether it's Redsox and Yankees, Patriots and Jets (even the Giants bumped their way into the mix defeating the then-perfect Patriots in Super Bowl XLII), or Celtics-Knicks from the late 60's and early 70's, those teams did not like each other and the hatred spilled into the fan base.

The more pronounced rivalry in the NBA was Boston-L.A. Two of the most storied franchises in the history of sports also had the honor of winning the most NBA championships of any NBA franchise. These teams also made practically every NBA Finals played in the 80's (Boston missed in 1983, 1988 & 1989, while the Lakers only missed out on the Finals in 1986 on a miracle shot by Ralph Sampson).

Magic Johnson and Larry Bird were the primary figures, but there were a host of future Hall-of-Famers in Kareem Abdul-Jabbar, James Worthy, Kevin McHale, Dennis Johnson and Robert Parish who got downright physical, knocking each other down, pushing, shoving, even clothes lining in one instance (Lakers forward Kurt Rambis was the unfortunate party at the wrong end of the wrestling move).

The Bad Boys of Detroit gave Chicago Bulls superstar Michael Jordan his share of lumps in the late '80s and early '90s when everyone was complaining about the "Jordan Rules", alleged favorable calls given to His Airness by referees because of his outstanding athletic ability.

There was no love lost in the Knicks-Bulls playoff matchups of the early 90s as the Patrick Ewing-led Knickerbockers staged epic playoff series from 1991-1993 with players like Charles Oakley, Anthony Mason, Xavier McDaniel, and John Starks all taking their shots at Jordan and Pippen but could not beat them in a series with Air Jordan on the roster.

At some point beginning with the aforementioned triumvirate of Garnett, Pierce and Allen, NBA players started to think if you can't beat 'em join 'em was the way to go.

With LeBron joining former Toronto Raptors All-Star Chris Bosh in Miami and Dwyane Wade, the Miami Heat all of a sudden became the most hated team in the league. I am almost positive the pep rally/coronation that ensued in American Airlines arena to introduce the new "Big 3" added to the vitriol from opposing fans.

Make no mistake, these new bad boys were great for the NBA. The new look Miami Heat reeled in the casual fan who may have only watched NBA games during the playoffs. People thought Miami didn't deserve this outrageous change of fortune because their fans were not as passionate about the Heat as other teams around the league. Miami has always been a football town with Heat games more of a place to be seen.

The coverage was relentless beginning with the first training camp live from a, wait for it, military base. With the world watching, the Heat led by the Big 3 did not disappoint. They took every team's best shot, LeBron finally vanquished the hated Boston Celtics, and went all the way to the NBA Finals.

Epilogue:

LeBron James spent the first season in Miami as one of the most hated individuals not only in the league, but in the world for the way he chose to leave the Cleveland Cavaliers. Although James seemed to outwardly embrace the role of villain, he would later admit that he stepped out of character trying to be a bad guy all of the time. James also admitted he would have handled his decision differently if given the opportunity.

This honesty with himself arguably freed his mind enough to concentrate on all things basketball, for in his second season with the Heat LeBron James would get the proverbial monkey off of his back by defeating the Oklahoma City Thunder in five games to secure his first NBA championship.

Hoisting the Larry O'Brien trophy served as vindication for James after failing to deliver in the Finals against the Dallas Mavericks the season before adding to the tremendous criticism he received in year one at Miami.

King James would add a second straight title to his crown in 2013 (year three), in a thrilling seven game series against The San Antonio Spurs, adding him to the rare list of back-to-back NBA champions.

Although he failed to three-peat in 2014, losing the rematch to the Spurs in five games, when you break it down, in four years in Miami LeBron has appeared in the NBA Finals four times, won twice, taken home two league MVP and two Finals MVP awards. This is exactly what he foresaw when he made his decision: the opportunity to win multiple championships.

Now LeBron has come full circle. Back with his hometown team with a legitimate chance at redemption and solidifying his status as a legend if he can win the city's first championship in any professional sport since 1964.

The only question was would the city of Cleveland take LeBron back after he got his rings somewhere else?

Hell yeah, if they were smart, and they are. He is still the best player in the world and still a few months removed from his 30th birthday. He has a point guard who can score in Kyrie Irving, an All-star big man in Kevin Love who is a double-double machine, and a bunch of great young talent acquired in the draft due to how bad they were without James.

LeBron going home again is great for the NBA, but it is still curious to me. Anderson Varejao is the only player left from the first LeBron era in Cleveland. Is it a coincidence that James came back now?

I think not… but that's just my thoughts.

Read the full statement below to see what LeBron was thinking during "The Decision 2.0":

 BY **LEBRON JAMES (AS TOLD TO LEE JENKINS)**

Posted: **Fri Jul. 11, 2014** Updated: **Sat Jul. 12, 2014**

Before anyone ever cared where I would play basketball, I was a kid from Northeast Ohio. It's where I walked. It's where I ran. It's where I cried. It's where I bled. It holds a special place in my heart. People there have seen me grow up. I sometimes feel like I'm their son.

Their passion can be overwhelming. But it drives me. I want to give them hope when I can. I want to inspire them when I can. My relationship with Northeast Ohio is bigger than basketball. I didn't realize that four years ago. I do now.

Remember when I was sitting up there at the Boys & Girls Club in 2010? I was thinking, This is really tough. I could feel it. I was leaving something I had spent a long time creating. If I had to do it all over again, I'd obviously do things differently, but I'd still have left. Miami, for me, has been almost like college for other kids. These past four years helped raise me into who I am. I became a better player and a better man. I learned from a franchise that had been where I wanted to go. I will always think of Miami as my second home. Without the experiences I had there, I wouldn't be able to do what I'm doing today.

*I went to Miami because of **D-Wade** and **CB**. We made sacrifices to keep **UD**. I loved becoming a big bro to **Rio**. I believed we could do something magical if we came together. And that's exactly what we did! The hardest thing to leave is what I built with those guys. I've talked to some of them and will talk to others. Nothing will ever change what we accomplished. We are brothers for life. I also want to thank Micky Arison and Pat Riley for giving me an amazing four years.*

I'm doing this essay because I want an opportunity to explain myself uninterrupted. I don't want anyone thinking: He and Erik Spoelstra didn't get along. … He and Riles didn't get along. … The **Heat** couldn't put the right team together. *That's absolutely not true.*

I'm not having a press conference or a party. After this, it's time to get to work.

When I left Cleveland, I was on a mission. I was seeking championships, and we won two. But Miami already knew that feeling. Our city hasn't had that feeling in a long, long, long time. My goal is still to win as many titles as possible, no question. But what's most important for me is bringing one trophy back to Northeast Ohio.

I always believed that I'd return to Cleveland and finish my career there. I just didn't know when. After the season, free agency wasn't even a thought. But I have two boys and my wife, Savannah, is pregnant with a girl. I started thinking about what it would be like to raise my family in my hometown. I looked at other teams, but I wasn't going to leave Miami for anywhere except Cleveland. The more time passed, the more it felt right. This is what makes me happy.

To make the move I needed the support of my wife and my mom, who can be very tough. The letter from Dan Gilbert, the booing of the Cleveland fans, the jerseys being burned -- seeing all that was hard for them. My emotions were more mixed. It was easy to say, "OK, I don't want to deal with these people ever again." But then you think about the other side. What if I were a kid who looked up to an athlete, and that athlete made me want to do better in my own life, and then he left? How would I react? I've met with Dan, face-to-face, man-to-

man. We've talked it out. Everybody makes mistakes. I've made mistakes as well. Who am I to hold a grudge?

*I'm not promising a championship. I know how hard that is to deliver. We're not ready right now. No way. Of course, I want to win next year, but I'm realistic. It will be a long process, much longer than it was in 2010. My patience will get tested. I know that. I'm going into a situation with a young team and a new coach. I will be the old head. But I get a thrill out of bringing a group together and helping them reach a place they didn't know they could go. I see myself as a mentor now and I'm excited to lead some of these talented young guys. I think I can help **Kyrie Irving** become one of the best point guards in our league. I think I can help elevate **Tristan Thompson** and **Dion Waiters**. And I* can't wait to reunite with **Anderson Varejao,** one of my favorite teammates.

But this is not about the roster or the organization. I feel my calling here goes above basketball. I have a responsibility to lead, in more ways than one, and I take that very seriously. My presence can make a difference in Miami, but I think it can mean more where I'm from. I want kids in Northeast Ohio, like the hundreds of Akron third-graders I sponsor through my foundation, to realize that there's no better place to grow up. Maybe some of them will come home after college and start a family or open a business. That would make me smile. Our community, which has struggled so much, needs all the talent it can get.

In Northeast Ohio, nothing is given. Everything is earned. You work for what you have.

I'm ready to accept the challenge. I'm coming home.

THE HUSBAND, THE FATHER, THE MENTOR
Dedicated to the memory of Douglas Lewis, Sr.

When I think about Douglas Lewis
senior/
the man with the inviting smile and
laid back demeanor/

selfless, devoted, so much more I can
say/
never afraid to put himself in harm's
way/

for his country, his wife his kids/
a man who would sacrifice in order to
give/

as a father he was ideal never ran out
on his duty/
to be a role model to his children what
a thing of beauty/

to be someone to look up to a man you
admire/
so much you want to do everything he
did or at least aspire/

to be just as noble, decent, humble,
stern/

confident that when he speaks you just
might learn/

something you never knew never acted
like he was above/
the next man matter of fact he was the
definition of love/

as a husband he was a lover, a friend
no doubt/
over 30 years of marriage still working
out/

jogging as a couple/
after her hard day of work he's waiting
to pick her up on the double/

as a mentor it was easy to follow the
lead/
of a man who gave you the tools to
build and also provided the keys/

I'd take his advice twice and come back
to hear it a third/
The epitome of respect a gentleman of
his word/

he's a man I want to be revered by both
sides of the family/
friends, colleagues, it's easy to ask
why did he leave/

Although his light was dimmed too soon/
he would not want us to be consumed/

with grief

because even though we don't see it he
feels relief/

Mr. Lewis is flashing that smile in the
presence of The Lord/
blessed with riches that money can't
afford/

see he was very much adored they say
the good go young/
he never abused his body yet this
scourge invaded his lungs/

God makes no mistakes so we can't call
this one/
let us rejoice in his time here easier
said than done/

although his physical form is gone his
legacy is unforgettable/

The Husband The Father, The Mentor The
Incredible

THE STOP

"Get your hands up and keep them where I can see them!"

On a dark, rainy night on the West Side Highway in New York City, two young men were at the wrong place at the wrong time. It was a mother's worst nightmare, especially if her son is a Black male in a nice car that happens to get pulled over by a police officer.

There were two police officers on this night, one to each side of the cranberry-colored Mercedes CL600, both with their guns drawn. The red, white and blue lights on top of the police car flashed like lasers, the headlights shone like megawatt beams so bright it illuminated the interior of the Mercedes.

Inside the two males could barely open their eyes to see the object of their interrogation. The young man behind the steering wheel is 21-year old Hakeem Griffin. His husky frame fills not only the unbuttoned black jeans jacket he is wearing, but the seat he is occupying even though it is slightly reclined. The strings from a tightly fitted wave cap protrude from underneath his navy blue baseball cap.

Hakeem is seemingly unfazed by the danger of the situation as if unfortunately he has either been here before or has been a witness to the repeated episodes in the reality TV of his environment.

His best friend Amani Johnson occupies the passenger seat. A little more mild-mannered in his gait, the severity of the situation is apparent on his face. The lines of worry pressed into his brow, lifting his eyelids and holding the corners of his mouth downward.

Amani had never had a gun pulled on him. He was brought up in a middle class home in a middle class section of Brooklyn. There was crime, but it was not as prevalent as in the more impoverished areas where numerous buildings as tall as the skyscrapers in Manhattan were called projects, which could have very well described the occupants.

All Amani wanted to do was pursue his dream of becoming a successful Hip Hop artist. He dedicated half of his life to achieving the goal. Less than an hour ago the two friends were in a nightclub where Amani had taken the stage to perform and called Hakeem out to join him.

Hakeem is also a rap artist, albeit a reluctant one at first.

His older brother Don introduced him to the world of Hip Hop as a youngster, but Hakeem never took it seriously. He wanted to play football. Still the pull of the music called him. Even when it wasn't paying early dividends, like any starving artist, he hustled to make ends meet.

Still, on this night Hakeem was very much into Hip Hop music, set on leaving his troubled past behind through the power of the boom bap and its control over a raucous crowd.

"Is there a problem, officer?"

There was a problem alright. Hakeem and Amani were driving in a fancy car late at night while being Black. It was a bad combination and when dealing with cops who were more of the *Boyz N' Da*

Hood variety than the ones on the old series that used to come on the FOX Network, it could be a deadly combination.

The traffic stop was on a visible stretch of road which is helpful yet, in this age of advanced technology where camera phones, bus lane cameras and surveillance cameras set atop local businesses can inadvertently capture criminal behavior or injustice, there are cops that still seem to get caught on tape demonstrating their own brand of justice.

At that moment another police cruiser rolled by. Amani watched as the white and blue vehicle taxied by the scene, fellow cops rubbernecking making sure their colleagues were okay. Amani's eyes moved from the officers to the side of the vehicle which read Courtesy Professionalism Respect with the first letter of each word in bold to spell out the acronym "C.P.R." He could only hope no one would be performing CPR on him or Hakeem on this night.

"Keep your hands where I can see them," said one of the officers. A burly White gentleman. Strands of salt and pepper hair peek out from underneath his police hat. With his right hand wrapped firmly around the handle of his gun, the officer is ready for any sudden movement, real or imagined.

"Do you know why we stopped you?" One cop asked.

Amani immediately looked over at Hakeem. As he suspected Hakeem's face contorted at what he perceived was the stupidity of the question. Amani knew that if two young black men would have any chance of leaving this situation unscathed he would have to keep Hakeem's mouth in check. This was not the time or place to be sarcastic or confrontational. Amani knew it, still...

"If we knew why you stopped us we wouldn't ask what the problem is now would we?"

The officer to Hakeem's left lowered his outstretched arms momentarily, no doubt stunned by the snide remark.

"Step out the car..."

"I ain't stepping out of shit!" Hakeem barked.

"Step out of the car!"

"Did I stutter?" Hakeem retorted.

Amani was amazed at how Hakeem was conducting himself with a gun in his face. Who knows how many young Black men these melanin-challenged twosome has stopped for driving while Black and, more importantly, how many have driven away under their own accord. Now here he was after arguably the best night of his life potentially minutes away from becoming a statistic.

"You think I'm playing with you, boy?"

"Boy?" Hakeem snapped turning his body in the seat toward the cop.

"Don't fucking move!"

"Maybe we should just do as they say, Ha," Amani offered.

Hakeem slowly twisted his head to Amani with a look of disgust.

"Are you out your fuckin mind?" Hakeem asked loud enough for the cops to hear.

"First of all these pigs haven't told me why I'm being pulled over."

"Speeding," one officer shouted.

"Speeding," Hakeem snarled twisting his head back to the steering wheel. "So we happen to be the only car on the west side highway driving a little faster than
the speed limit the entire night?"

"Stop running your mouth and get out of the car!"

"You ain't even ask for my license and registration. You ain't even gonna check if my shit is legit. You just want to go straight to the ass whipping? Fuck y'all we ain't getting out this muthafuckin car!

The officer standing slightly behind Hakeem's left shoulder removes his right hand from his weapon reaches into the window and grabs Hakeem by the back of the neck and slams his head into the steering wheel.

"What the fuck are you doing?" a stunned Amani yells.

"Shut the fuck up and get out of the car like my partner said" screams the cop standing behind Amani.

Amani looks at Hakeem whose head remains buried in the steering wheel. His right arm is barely visible his right hand not so much. He is clearly reaching for something. Amani's eyes widen. He has to think quickly. If he allows Hakeem to make a sudden move they will surely die in the car they are sitting in.

"This is bullshit!" Amani screams keeping perfectly still as to not give the cops a reason to discharge their weapons. "Y'all still can't tell us what we did
to be deserving this treatment right now!" he continued.

"Why are we being subjected to this? We are minding our own business, not harassing anyone."

Hakeem starts to raise his arm a little faster. Amani shifts his left hand slightly discreetly grabbing Hakeem's wrist and pins it to the side of his leg.

"Let my hand go," Hakeem demands in a hurried whisper.

Amani ignores his request and continues to work on the cops.

"We are two hardworking guys trying to make an honest living!" Amani shoots Hakeem a desperate look through widened eyes as to warn his friend 'don't do this'. Hakeem is already gone. He has been embarrassed and now abused.

Hakeem starts to move his right arm vigorously trying to shake free of Amani's grip. The longer Amani holds on the more aggressive Hakeem's movements to extricate his arm. Amani, fearful that any detection of movement could trigger the two cops, removes his hand from Hakeem's wrist. Hakeem in turn directs a nasty glare at Amani who returns it with a look of resignation.

Amani shifts his head slightly to the right to face forward. Slowly closing his eyes, he breathes inward then exhales a deep breath of exasperation. How did he go from performing on stage in front of hundreds of people to being pulled over on a lonely stretch of the West Side Highway staring down the barrel of a gun? A casualty of a war he wanted no part of.

Amani opens his eyes. Through his peripheral vision he can see Hakeem raising his arm revealing a piece of cold black steel. A 9mm pistol. He knew Hakeem owned a gun, he just didn't think his hotheaded friend would be dumb enough to carry it in his vehicle. His mind starts to race, thinking about the people he will never see again: his mother, his sister, the cousin that inspired him to do music.

Hakeem's eyes are trained on his side mirror where the reflection of the officer and his gun is in plain view, fixed on him, index finger pressed against the trigger waiting for a cue to move inward and make another young Black male extinct.

Unlike Amani, his mind is trapped in the present. There is no thought of future repercussions like jail or death. He is not thinking about the personal and emotional toll this irrational decision will have on his mother and older brother. He is blinded by rage, seething with anger, consumed by a fury to enact his own form of justice against the very people hired and compensated with tax payer dollars to serve and protect.

Hakeem's hand began trembling with the anticipation not that different from performing in front of an audience. As he slowly raised his weapon beads of sweat began to form on his face. His reflexes would have to be cat-like to catch the cop off guard. Still he had to know that even if he hit the cop, the officer with his gun trained on Amani would immediately fire his weapon in response.

And for just a moment, pride gave way to common sense. Hakeem's right arm halted its ascent, remarkably still out of view of the two cops. The outline of his jawbone began to show repeatedly through both sides of his face as he gritted his teeth through clenched lips. The thought of letting these boorish boys in blue get their way infuriated him.

"We have a code 13 officer in distress…"

Hakeem's right arm froze in place. Amani's eyes grew wider. He looked to his left and right without moving his head. He trained his eyes on his side view mirror. The officer immediately withdrew his weapon and looked over at his partner.

The cop on Hakeem's side continued to train his weapon on his target apparently oblivious to the transmitted alert of a colleague in peril.

"Charlie!" yelled the officer on Amani's side attempting to gain the attention of the otherwise distracted comrade.

"Charlie, we gotta go!"

"Shut up, Bobby!"

The transmission blares across the police radio a second time. Charlie does not move. Amani, thinking the ordeal was over, closes his eyes again. Apparently they attracted a cop who cares nothing about his fellow officers being in trouble. He turns his head slightly to the left when he notices movement.

Apparently Hakeem is aware that this cop is not going anywhere. His right arm begins slowly moving upwards again.

"Charlie - "

"Stop yelling my fucking name! I'm not going anywhere until we are done here!"

Clearly frustrated, Bobby holsters his weapon and races back to the squad car. Amani keeps an eye on his movements through the rear view mirror. Thankfully one of these cops realizes valuable time is being wasted here.

Charlie remains laser focused on Hakeem like he has collared a fugitive. Who knows what is happening to the officer in need of assistance somewhere in another area of New York yet this grizzled proponent of integrity feels his priority is with two young Black men who have done nothing to threaten anyone's safety - yet.

Amani's eyes close and fly open at the sound of an ignition. He looks up at the rear view mirror. Officer Bobby has started the police cruiser apparently ready to respond to the distress call.

Officer Charlie finally breaks his statuesque stance and turns in the direction of his partner.

"Shit!" he grunts as he reluctantly starts over to the moving squad car.

This is the distraction Hakeem needed. He uses his left hand to open his door. With a half twist of his upper body, he is facing the officers, most importantly Charlie. His right arm swings around to the forefront. His arm extends with the shiny black steel in plain view pointing in the direction of his oppressor.

With a steady arm and thick index finger hugging the trigger the transmission of a second distress call is mere seconds from materializing.

"HAKEEM!" Amani cries out into the still night.

Bullet.

WHAT UP, POP?

What up, Pop?
A term of endearment in the inner city/
a replacement for Daddy in the era of
Diddy/

cuz daddy is like a curse word in the
hood/ whenever it was heard it was
never good/

deadbeat sperm donor irresponsible
intimacy/ birthed a generation of
illegitimate seeds/

that grow to hate their surname/ so
instead of living with the ghost of
invisible expectations they play the
word game/

use my middle name unless it's my
daddy's/ then forget it exists just
like daddy/

instead we call to our boy on the
corner/ the name reserved for the only
man that should learn us right from
wrong —

What up, Pop?

I ain't talking about soda/ The dudes that only come around once a month like they got a quota/

throwing money around on cars and clothes but don't wanna grow their daughter/ who should be the sun in the life of their sons but don't have an aorta/

the reason why our sons ain't living to see a quarter/ of their life expectancy – see they expect we to fail/ and we are by turning to violent families and turning up in jail/

turning in a cell cuz you turnt up/ but ain't got nobody to turn up wit bail/

the same time we turn away from our youth/ we justify making them prey to the boys in blue/

who ask questions after they shoot/ then send another wave after we loot/

what life can you save by protesting in peace/ when the next child falls victim to the beast/

and you can't get a name of the pig who
killed an innocent soul/ or convict the
prick using illegal chokeholds/

but they quick to release the pic of
the four that vandalized the store/ and
the deceased shoplifting in a video -

but Mike Brown has a dad and Eric
Garner took care of six/ so how can we
blame the man or dirty politics/

still it feels like the game's been
fixed - I fear my eight year old
may get caught up in the mix/

of someone who feels he can't be on a
certain block/ a pat frisk after a
profile stop/ where one false move real
or imagined
can lead to - *POP*

What up, Pop?

I ain't talking 'bout corn/ 23 years
since you moved on/ with a new breed
from your mistress/ been three since
you been gone and I still remember
those empty speeches at that funeral
home blink and you missed it/

forced to reminisce of a blissful
experience/ I surely took for granted
cuz no way would my dad be supplanted/

no way My superman who I thought cock
diesel/ Drove off didn't look back
didn't stop and Pop - goes the weasel

Now I'm mad/ mad at dad nope - not for
speeding away/ and not looking back
that day but for giving me hope/

don't call my house looking for me if
you can't talk to my momma/ is what I
shoulda said but I was unaware of the
drama/

all I knew was he was on the other end
of the phone/ talking about how he
coming home

How many years am I gonna mourn/ before
I snap out of the fog and realize he's
gone/

but now he's back not physical but in
me/ now that I have my own seeds/

to water I have to be an example for my
son and daughter/ I gotta pass a torch
that almost led me to slaughter/

I gotta be a man when I wasn't taught
a/ damn thing when it mattered most /

my teen years I was missing a James
Avery/ still I stayed fresh in the face
of mental slavery/

I wore the mask some mistaken for
bravery/ all became clear to me once I
started singing the ABCs/

to my mini me I grew up as a person
exponentially/ I knew I couldn't stand
for being someone unsavory/

so I'll be damned if they ever walk up
and say to me…

What up, Pop?

RHYME FINATIC: FROM JAYSKI TO J.I.M. FLOW

Opening:
2005 was the last year I put out music to this point. It was also the year I got married. Coincidence? I felt as a married man not achieving my ultimate goal as a musician it was time to explore other avenues of being a success in entertainment. At the time I was pursuing a Master's degree in Media Arts with a concentration in screenwriting so naturally since I spent more than half my life trying to be a Hip Hop artist I felt it was time to move onto screenwriting. A true artist never really retires, however. In this chapter I decided to pull out the time machine and share some of my old rap lyrics.

RAP NAME: JAYSKI

UNTITLED (1987)

This was the first rhyme I ever wrote in life. I was motivated by my older cousin Anthony "Oliver" Hall who was rhyming under the pseudonym *T-Unique*. He was a proponent of the golden age Hip Hop of the time and was as nice with the wordplay as Rakim, Big Daddy Kane or Kool G Rap. Influenced by my cousin and the aforementioned artists and Run-DMC, I went home and penned the following:

Jayski is my name and I'm number one/
MC's on the mic they just want to
front/
but the rhymes I say come out fresh and
clean/
better than the other rappers on the
scene/
def cut creator behind the turntables/
man-free girls just willing and able/
rockin' on the mic with a hot rank 1/
the hot ranking days have just begun/
I'm funky fresh stone cold rap supreme/
and that's what the beautiful ladies
all dream- about

After this I honed my skills writing rhymes for a fictional group I fashioned after Run-DMC. What an imagination, huh? It wasn't until I got to middle school in 1989 that I started to focus on my own material. First I had to change my name. It was about to be the start of the 90s. No one had a "Ski" attached to their name anymore. I started going by **"Tress"** at one point. Don't ask me what the name means or how I came up with it. I don't even know. It took me a few weeks to come to my senses and return to **Jayski** until further notice.

BE FLY OR DIE (1991)

Remember when emcees made songs with four verses (i.e. Eric B. & Rakim *"Know The Ledge"*, LL Cool J *"Bad"*)? Now rappers can barely put two verses together without an R&B singer on the track. Somewhere Q-Tip is rolling over his drum machine (peep A Tribe Called Quest's *"The Low End Theory"* for some choice words against the meshing of Hip Hop and R&B). This song was actually a response to a battle I was in with one of my intermediate school friends. If I could have written four more verses I would, I was that angry. It wasn't until years later I found out the guy was using lyrics from Masta Ace. Below is the first verse.

Plain and simple as the shoes on your feet/
when I'm on the mic suckers (remember when rappers called each other suckers?) *take a back seat/*
cuz I'm the only one sure to make you nervous/
make the elderly and handicapped sit up and take notice/

I'm like the type to make you kick back/
my rhymes supreme not slack so drop that/
I rap smooth on a mellow tempo/
a rhyme terminator suckers say hello/
to the end of your career cuz I'm here/
I obsess possess I manifest a nightmare/
pure domination is what I stand for/
break ya like a bone rip through ya like a chainsaw/
I'm so unique competition can't stand much/
crumble under pressure can't stand up to the bumrush/
the mic is my blender and suckers I'll liquefy/
the message I'm sending is clear be fly or die

RAP NAME: RAGE

GIMME DA MIC (1993)

In the fall of 1992 I decided to join three other guys I met during my freshman year of high school and form a rap group named Styles May Vary (S.M.V.). It was the first time I knew I had to step my rap game up because I was not the lone voice on a song anymore. I wanted to have the best verse on every track we did and as a result my lyrical content got progressively better. I changed my name to **Rage** at this time. We were going to a house studio and recording our own raps over other people's tracks. This song was done to the instrumental to Shaquille O'Neal's "What's Up Doc" featuring The Fushnickens. We would make tapes and pass it out around the school. The reaction made us feel like we were really gonna come out and get signed, but of course it is never that easy. It was a great time in our lives though. I know I have those tapes somewhere.

It's a funky sensation when the steel gets gripped/
n!ggas start to call me Shredder cuz of mics I ripped/
cuz I show nuff skill and still be skillin' when I break/
with a hundred percent flavor free from the mistakes/
come equipped with the gift of gab when I rip/
don't slip cuz I'm ko styling from the psycho tip/
I get mad and take it out on the microphone/

from the constant rhyming I start to go
in a zone/
the words keep flowing cuz Rage never
quits/
you say oh sh*t when the funky flyboy
hits/
I do my thing at a show then I part
with the dough/
I laugh (Elmer Fudd laugh) at your
Elmer Fuddy Duddy flow/
first in the collaboration/
of three styles looking for fan
appreciation/
chew punks up like Mike and Ike/
then in turn do more of what you like
when you gimme da mic

YA GET DONE (1994)

I was still in the group S.M.V. at this time. In the last year of
"The Golden Age" I was all about showing skills and showcasing
my wordplay. These three verses below stood out on their
respective songs.

*I enter the stage drop rhymes like a
bomb/*
*watch wack MC's fall like scuds from
Saddam/*
*on a certain area seek and destroy like
a terrier/*

my hype styles spread like motherfu@%!ng malaria/
I bury ya with my ill sh*t then spit on your gravesite/
and still keep the groove in the heart like Dee Lite/
explode like dynamite untouchable like Elliot Ness/
step in a jam blow up the spot like David Koresh*/
play like a pimple break out my skills spread out to DC/
CD's TV all the way to WKRP/
flip sh*t like a spatula my skills spectacular/
send ya home you start biting off more heads than Dracula/
punks bring beef I'm fu@%!n USDA/
bring the noise my way your rhymes I'll slay like Santa/
kick something fly then motherfu@%ers wanna flee/
they styles Slimfast my sh!t is fu@%!n obesity/
or fatness I'll show the world like an Atlas/
how it goes n!ggas get done like five dollar hoes

*David Koresh was the guy that set the infamous fire that burned down an entire compound in Waco, Texas and became a popular punchline in the process.

SKILLS UPON STYLES (1994)

*My skills is deep like an abyss the
rhyme terrorist/
when the mic touch my hand I start
metamorphosis/
if you know not yet who I be/
MBF after a battle I'm left over like
debris/
known to cause catastrophes when I
smoke like Phillies/
leaving punks more physically
challenged than muscular dystrophy/
I be the ill man the one you want man/
wit skills and don't front man or I'll
burn that ass like a suntan/
nowhere near Charles but I can be a
real dickens/
leave my rhyme pad in the garbage so
the lines will be kickin'/
words I freak it drop beats I skill it/
no friends I beg frying suckers in a
skillet like eggs/
get open like eyes witness the skills
like Jehovah/
when I flow I flood the stage so n!ggas
boat (remember when cats said "boat" to
mean scram or beat it?) like Noah/
got suckers catchin' fits when I get
ridiculous/
my metaphors got the devil saying 'the
hell with this'/*

I be the MB play ya like a CD/
coolin' like AC releasing more deadly
rays than UV/
call in the army and I'll be all I can
be/
lyrically non-believers get cut like
Oregami/
I gets stupid but I'm an intellectual/
ya dis and I'll be back on dat ass like
a bisexual/
here I come like bust nuts I leave
blood wit my cuts/
call me cigarette butts cuz I be
smoking' n!ggas

UNTITLED (RANDOM VERSE) (1994)

I wrote a lot of these random verses and if they found a place in one of my songs so be it. This was a time when rappers were innovative and not scared to be creative with concepts in their work, which is one of the reasons I fell in love with Hip Hop in the first place. I took my stab at rapping in alliterations here.

I be the fabulous funk freaka flippin'
phat tracks for ages/
the satisfying sound hit slowly when I
step on stages/
this mad man makes a madder man more
madder/
by ripping records with rhymes sweet
like pitter patter/

of little feet big feet I get ferocious/
fly rhymes gets feedback from fans keeping Finatic in focus/
never shy when I sound out pound out serious skills serving suckers/
I leave my mark like a stamp on n!ggas so hit the showers/
like a baseball player when ejected/
like Peter I pick rhymes put it down when it's perfected/
my persona puts punks in a petrified state/
scared straight no survivors/
my sounds startle leaving suckers dripping saliva/
from dropped lips lyrically lively letting loose vocally/
laid back sh*t looming large worldwide and locally/
the legend my menacing masterpieces are more/
superior style leave suckers sh!tt!n' in their drawers/
no flaws fill the flow I freak fu@k!ng heads up when I speak/
wastin' warriors waxing wack wimps for weeks

N.U.T.S. (1994)
(Never Underestimate The Skills)

This was supposed to be a posse cut featuring the seven rhyming members of our high school crew that never materialized. Everyone had their verses yet the song was never recorded, one of many missed opportunities.

You do not want to see what I have up my sleeve/
wack MC's get turned over like a new leaf/
unique technique I'm elite swinging hits in different strokes like Phillip Drummond/
the wickedness is coming/
ya soft like ice cream I come to give the licks/
pour cement in your body and have you sh!tt!n' bricks/
battles are in vain I set in like stains/
ni&&as rhymes couldn't stand up if they had a fu@k!n' cane/
I go on a tear I wear rhymes like new gear/
catch stares from my peers kick MC's in the rear/
Finatic got more tricks than that cereal Lord/
my styles are full grown you still on the umbilical cord/

with the provisions rhymes are made like decisions/
comp couldn't meet me head on in a collision/
MC's get beat down like initiations/
creations leave you seeing more stars than constellations/
comp no wins Mind Blowing the veteran/
step in the end zone and get spiked like pigskin/
the terror dome I eat up ozones like Styrofoam/
your rhymes are coming out more busted than silicone

In 1994 Styles May Vary went from four to a two man group, myself and my partner Naim "Bleek" Rivera. With the emergence of The Lady of Rage on the West coast, I changed my rap name from Rage to Mind Blowing Finatic (M.B.F.). We made small inroads as a duo, most notably getting invited in the studio to record with the legendary group Full Force. We recorded verses for a song called "Can I Get Your Number". We got bumped off the final cut for a group they were producing called "Screem", but it was a learning experience nonetheless.

RAP NAME: MIND BLOWING FINATIC (M.B.F.)

HERE COMES THE FINATIC (1999)

Five years into my solo mission I went away to Baltimore to attend Morgan State University and came back to Brooklyn still trying to make a living off of Hip Hop. As I continued to evolve in my sound and style I started to focus on making real songs with actual hooks. This was one of the first in a wave of what I thought were "radio-friendly" songs.

Let your eyes awaken I got juice like Orangina/
although I never shake in mic arena confrontations/
when I stick my face in crews hold shit up like constipation/
my mind activation conjure more lyrics than Jason/
without Jada swift delivery like newspapers/
that'll turn eager MC's into procrastinators/
got shit hemmed it seems (seams)
million dollar smile when teeth gleam/
rhyme for days recruit the illest on my team/
then hit the court rhyming's the sport that gets the cream/
I got conceited motherfu@kers losing self-esteem/
the mind beam take you to different worlds like Kadeem/

*create rhymes in the crib that'll bump
in the street/
a capella or with beat/
I freak the underground level but still
keep sh!t concrete my battle
techniques/
will take you back like retro ni&&as I
train like metro/
I'm new but my wordplay rank with some
of the best though/
my flow's master locked run through
solo or combination/
got your girl looking at me like I was
Mason*/
keep your heart racing when mics touch
my lips/
gave y'all a few minutes to shine now
prepare for the eclipse.*

*Mason Betha, also known as Bad Boy recording artist Ma$e

*Hook: I got a beef with the rhythm
beats I step to it/ the mic is my
accomplice lyrics I prep to shoot it/
load up the artillery hold crews for
ransom/embarrass y'all like Hilary*
leave the crime scenery/ stage left
even with no snags/ my style will turn
y'all riches into rags/ tired of too
much wack in your ear drum/ here comes
Finatic extracting 'em.*

*A reference to then-First Lady Hilary Clinton being
embarrassed by the Monica Lewinsky scandal involving her

husband President Bill Clinton that was still making news at the time

SHOW LOVE (2000)

I was very angry on this track, feeling slighted by the lack of respect I felt I deserved for being a good lyricist. Never mind the fact that I wasn't doing any shows or promoting my music on a consistent basis at the time, I couldn't believe no one was trying to sign me. Hey, the best music is made when you're upset. Just ask LL Cool J, Eminem or Nas.

Put the needle to the groove and start this/
Mind Blowing steps through the darkness mind state is heartless/
to half-assed artists given the chance to shine and surpass this artist/
but their rhymes got no chance against mine regardless/
trying to gain credit but can't face the charges/
skills you lack – weak attempts garbage get blocked like Marcus/
Camby leave more nicks than the Garden/
on suspect chins there's no closing the margin/
when I'm out the box similar to Mike Johnson/
drill it into your noggin I'm sick like Parkinson/
stance never soften scrubs never endorsing/
new acts wack all they know about is flossin'/

*damn right I'm playa hating there's no
skills offering/
worked too hard and too long/
to see niggas use relatives to get on*

LET OFF STEAM (2003)

My last ditch efforts to become a professional Hip Hop artist began here with the release of my first mixtape *"Upstart Mixtape: 2K3 Sh!t"*. This was the season of 50 Cent and G-Unit's mixtape takeover and I, like many rappers at the time, jumped on the bandwagon.

*I be the unsung veteran out for light
like Edison/
dudes talking 'bout getting cake
sweeter than Entemanns/
make wack rappers keep walking like Ce
Peniston/
wit a flow that bring house calls and
lots of medicine/
reppin' BK swing it all the way down to
Maryland/
brother you would recommend virtually
better than/
cats talking 'bout seeing me ain't in
my sights/
I come on the scene they scramble like
the QB of the Vikes (Vikings)/
Culpepper the hot stepper like Ini
(Kamoze)/
got a fetish for pretty toes and big
hineys/*

you got beef I bring the lettuce temper fiery/
to rappers out of line won't get the best of me like Mya/
be the track arsonist microphones keep sparking it/
peeps calling me out from 106 and Park/
and it's been over two years leave my mark it appears/
people ain't heard of me I'm slowly catching their ear

Hook:
One two One two yes yes it's me/
The rap prodigy by the name of MB/
when I'm stressed grab the m-i-c let off steam/ build up a buzz in the street and touch cream/
One two One two yes yes the rhyme maker/ sick wit the lines it's time to catch a break/ I put it on paper/ hit the lab put it on haters/ put it on greater my presence felt sooner or later

CHANGE FLOWZ (2005)

I had a little fun over the *"Change Clothes"* beat. This joint is on the sequel to the first mixtape. The *"Upstart 2"* mixtape, released in 2005, would be my last recorded work to this point.

Ya boy is back Upstart 2 new raps/
got a couple from 1 in fact/
ain't no question MB can rap y'all
sleepin/
it's time to wake the land up execs put
grands up/
props I snatch grab them my pick in the
draft/
uno - king Jay like a Cleveland Cav
(LeBron!)/
when this rap anomaly dispatch a
paragraph/
I'm like a bad economy dismiss your
staff/
nowadays you hear talk about artists
that leave/
I'm trying to spit on songs with my
favorite artists then leave/
hear my music know I'm one call away
like J Weav(er)/
Chingy - dimes fight for me pulling out
they weave/
cuz the kid spit hardest flows is on
target/
blaze stage shows wit more fire than
reggae artists/

*BA in English don't make me the
smartest/
still I grew up on Special Ed wordplay
retarded*

SHOW ME SOME LOVE (2005)

Okay I went against the grain on this joint. My homey Dre Black out of Washington D.C. was singing on the hook and had a verse, but the track was so unbelievable I had to jump on it. It was a sign of the times in Hip Hop that the songs that were getting extensive radio play had an R&B artist on the hook. I was not one to follow trends. I had real faith in Dre Black and my homegirl Cindy came in with the R&B and jazz scat blend. I was pushing this song heavy in my final effort to get some recognition.

*Show me some XOXO/
rhymes on point like 32 gold and purple
(Magic!) presto change-o/
how my lines form like I got a personal
angel/
guiding me got the ladies with their
heart on they sleeve/
got a lot of practice serving MC's and
taking sets/
now the U.S. Open unsung vet/
remember when I was a young un hoping
to get in the league/
now a lot of heads scoping the rap J
Weav (that's two Jason Weaver
references!)/
yo I'm one call away/*

*and just know I got candy for your ear
like everyday Valentine's Day/
the way I'm murdering this track I'm
putting flowers on graves/
she got her eyes on my ice like I made
a beautiful save (hockey!)/
I share the wealth don't need the optic
attacks/
let's all live you feeling the track
it's All Hizz/
I see your head nodding cuz your neck
know/
the kid's got mad skills (Mad Skillz)
stop the hating time to show - me some*

YES SIR (2005)

This free rhyme off of the *Upstart 2* mixtape was how I was getting down at the time. It was all hands on deck, a final haymaker. I am proud of both *Upstart* mixtapes. I've been out of the lab for almost 10 years, but as they say a true artist never quits. I gave up the name Mind Blowing Finatic because I learned the acronym is connected to gang related activity, something I do not associate with. The next time I release music the "mind blowing" will still be a part of my name in some capacity.

*What's da deal man yo I throw darts
with skill man/
some of y'all look the part but can't
ball like Hill* man/
put me on the bill man I cop them bills
man/*

different cities different worlds I school rappers like Hillman/
with no Bonet serve em like entrees/
wicked wordplay flow like Bobby Bouche (waterboy!)/
toss me to the side thinking I'll go away/
but when I come back around it get ugly like Strange/
the game getting old lotta rappers going away/
they like Jay you getting old rap throw it away/
take it in over (Ali)ze or some blue juice/
trying to take me out my spot y'all funny n!ggas like Bruce Bruce/
what I look like retiring I'm colder than off irons/
no Usher - light it up like faulty wiring/
never sloppy hit shelves make sure you cop me/
my mask off running 'round like somebody stop me/
I'm a giant like a chicks wit tight ends Jeremy Shockey/
y'all know the routine get big chicks wanna co@k me/
haters slow your roll please don't get cocky/

*I'll leave seeds on your b!t@h buns
that's not poppy/
how the cream spill out/
you an amateur sticking your chest out
n!gga you still need to fill out/
trends I buck it/
make hits for radio but follow the
block like TJ Duckett/
Jacob Technician Movado the watch fu@k
it/
spoil myself wit hot gear name brand
bucket/
Kenneth Cole over the optics/
unsung juggernaut when the loco in
motion you can't stop it/
you know the kid make moves like
choreographers/
make a lot of d!ckheads beat it like
pornographers/
cranberry Benzito it's Pablito/
dope spitter that flip birds and spread
eagles/
n!ggas got a lot of hubris I dead egos/
take away they drive like I snatched
they vehicle/
the stage is Tokyo on any night/
n!ggas call me Buster Douglas the way I
hit mikes*

*Former NBA superstar Grant Hill was going through what
would later be discovered to be life threatening issues with his
ankle which caused him to miss a lot of games as a member of
the Orlando Magic.

Closing:

My last live performance was March 28, 2006. I performed a medley of two songs at a showcase in Manhattan. After I was done, I put the microphone down and walked away from the stage for the last time to this point. It was time to move on to other endeavors in my quest to live comfortably as a creative artist. I had gone back to graduate school to pursue a degree in Media Arts with a concentration in screenwriting and, inspired by my classroom studies, I started writing screenplays. I entered screenwriting competitions and soon realized that, like the music industry, the film industry was a field that was very challenging and required tireless dedication to the craft. My graduate thesis required I submit a screenplay based on my topic, but ironically it would be the subject of my thesis that would inspire me to write my debut book "Pass The Torch: How A Young Black Father Challenges The Deadbeat Dad Stereotype".

JUST MY THOUGHTS...

The title of this book of short stories and poetry is based on a tagline I use to end many of the entries on my blog: "W.R.E.a.C Havoc Thoughts of the Day". So I figure it is only right to end with some of my most opinionated posts for those who have or have not visited the site. Please check out the following posts and more at www.wreachavoconline.blogspot.com

Tuesday June 17, 2008 (first entry)

Welcome to My Thoughts...

I would like to take the time to welcome everyone who has and will visit my blog. It is what I envision will be the beginning of a myriad of written content released from the W.R.E.a.C Havoc umbrella. With this blog I aim to share my "opinion based on facts", to utilize my creative resources in this forum to construct innovative, informed, and cutting edge content geared towards making a dynamic impact in the world of music, film, publishing, sports, fashion, politics, and popular culture, without prejudice, or personal bias.

With that said, there is no me without

you the reader. I encourage you to visit, interact, agree, disagree, post your thoughts and let your voice be heard on this site. I will do my best to engage all commentary positive or negative within reason.

Thank you again for taking time out of your day and remember,

These are just my thoughts ladies and gentlemen....

Posted by Jamiyl Samuels at 7:57 PM

Happy Father's Day

This past Sunday, June 15th 2008, was my second Father's Day. I want to wish all the fathers and social fathers (i.e. uncles, brothers, etc. taking on a paternal role) who actively participate in their children's lives a Happy Father's Day. Thanks for being responsible! Know that your presence in your child's life is very important and does make an impact on their future development.

Fatherhood in the African-American community, with a focus on the stereotype of deadbeat dads, was the subject of my graduate thesis and is

very personal for me. My father left
the family when I was 10 years old and
it motivated me to be the total
opposite.

I want to take the time to thank my
Mother for being my father as well. I
want to thank my wife Tracy-Ann for
giving me the gift of a child to be a
father to.
I want to thank my son for inspiring me
to be the best Father I can be.

If you are a father who loves your
child(ren), have a father who you
admire, or experienced a childhood
without your father, let it be known
right here.

Peace and Love!

Posted by Jamiyl Samuels at 8:42 PM

Is Obama being set up?

It still hasn't hit me that an African-
American man is the Democratic
candidate for The President of the
United States of America. Though Obama
has done his best to downplay the
obligatory racial undertones that have
seeped into his campaign, I can't help
but look at how far Blacks have come as

158

a people. Forget about slavery from centuries past for a moment, only because that is an obvious analogy. Look at the last 40 years! Look what the Black Panthers had to go through, Rosa Parks, Dr. Martin Luther King, Jr. died 40 years ago for this moment to come to fruition. Numerous Black leaders, abolitionists, innovators, and the like have written about the treatment of Blacks by the majority and their desire for the need for racial equality.

With that said, we have had people allude to talk of assassination (none on a President or candidate since Ronald Reagan was shot at almost 30 years ago), even Hillary Clinton (with her remark about Robert Kennedy when asked about conceding the race to Obama). I have heard whispers from the Carribean community in Brooklyn that Obama's nomination is too good to be true, that the powers that be have conspired to allow Obama to win the nomination because it would be easier for John McCain to get elected. The thought is that the people of the United States of America would never elect a Black President.

While I try not to give talk like this credence, looking at the failed attempts to run for President in the past by the likes of Jesse Jackson and Al Sharpton, Barack Obama's monumental ride is important, refreshing, and in my opinion based on the country's real desire for change.

I wouldn't go as far to believe Barack Obama is being set up, I have faith in the American people (I may be naive) that those who support Obama believe he is the best chance the country has to begin to change what has taken place the last eight years.

Just my thoughts ladies and gentlemen...

What do you think?

Posted by Jamiyl Samuels at 10:29 PM

Wednesday June 18, 2008

Celtics win convincingly... to put it mildly

I'm a Knicks fan (don't feel sorry for me...we'll be back), but I must say the Celtics showed why they were the best team in the NBA with a convincing (to be nice) win over the Los Angeles Lakers in Game 6 to take the NBA title and earn a 17th championship banner for Beantown.

This was such a thorough thrashing, I almost expect Kobe Byant to demand a trade in the post game press conference. It ain't that easy without Shaq, Kobe.

Why do I feel Shaq is somewhere smiling? "Yes, he can't win one without me."

I'm trying to rewind my TiVo to the beginning of the game so I can record it.

I'm happy for Kevin Garnett, Paul Pierce, and Ray Allen - they won the title so now they can officially be called "The Big Three". Before tonight I couldn't understand why people put that pressure on those guys. Larry Bird, Robert Parish, and Kevin McHale earned that moniker. Now "Three Amigos" can claim the name.

Good job by whoever was pushing the bleep button on ABC, especially when

ABC sideline reporter Michelle Tafoya
attempted to interview KG at the end of
the game. Maybe I should commend tape
delay because KG's F word outburst
would have caught me totally off guard.

It's OK Boston, the Knicks will be
there next year... what? It's not 2010?

Just my thoughts....

Posted by Jamiyl Samuels at 12:49 AM

Saturday June 21, 2008

An "Untitled" Album vs. the "N"
I was on the train and I heard a
Caucasian guy call an Asian guy the "N"
word. I wasn't trying to listen to
their conversation (besides the fact
they were talking about nothing). They
were loud and the "N" word is what
caught my attention. I didn't know
whether to be outraged or laugh at how
stupid the comment was.

The "N" word has a lot of negative
connotations associated with African
Americans, but rap music has conveyed
the message that it is okay to call
each other the "N" word under the guise
of taking back the power of the word

from the white man. Nonsense. I'm guilty of using the word towards others, however only when speaking about ignorant Black men. Let's face it, slaves were uneducated for the most part and they were called the "N" word regularly in a condescending tone.

Actually, I still don't know when Latinos got the go ahead to call each other the "N" word. I'm assuming because Latinos are considered a minority they have embraced the term... whatever (whenever I hear Fat Joe say the "N" word I cringe - look at the criticism J-Lo got for saying the "N" word in "Ain't It Funny" [thanks a lot Ja Rule]).

Nas wanted to name his upcoming album the "N" Word (actually "Hip Hop Is Dead" was supposed to be called the "N" Word, instead Nas made a clever play with words calling the last part of the title "The N [End]"). Now the album title has been changed to "Untitled" due to outcry from label executives. What happened to freedom of speech? If anyone can pull off an "N" word titled album it's Nas. After all he was the first to rap a song about being a gun (I Gave You Power) on his second album, and every song on Illmatic is thought-provoking.

Back to the white guy and the Asian on the train. As they continued to talk to each other like rappers, I thought to myself something has to be done about the casual use of the "N" word. Rappers have to step up and set some boundaries if they are gonna continue to rap every other word with "N".

I don't ever want to be witness to what I heard on the train again. it's just wrong. It's wrong for rappers, and plain civilians to call each other that, but we've become so immune that people from other races feel it's okay to use the "N" word.

Don't let me get started on what African Americans could be saying to each other that would offend Caucasians, Asians, and Latinos. Think of it that way my fellow people of a different race. You wouldn't want Blacks calling each other "cracker" or "j*p" or "sp*c" in regular conversation.

Just my thoughts...

Posted by Jamiyl Samuels at 12:21 AM

Tuesday June 24, 2008

Shaq Attacks!

I believe I mentioned in a previous post after the Celtics won the title that Shaq was somewhere smiling. Well he was somewhere freestyling. Showing that he still has animosity for Kobe, Shaq asked number 24, formerly number 8, to tell him how is anus tasted on stage in a night club this past Sunday (6/22/08). Tell 'em how you really feel, Shaq! "Kobe ratted me out that's why I'm getting divorced" Ouch. Then in the next line he says he would never give a woman a million dollars in hush money.

Okay, but you just said Kobe ratted you out. If you didn't do it, he couldn't rat you out.

Moving on... It's funny, but it's sad. Let's hope Kobe doesn't come out with a response rap (remember that awful song with Tyra Banks... where he was rapping in Italian???).

See the hilarious video here http://www.tmz.com/tmz_main_vide o?titleid=1626146951

Posted by Jamiyl Samuels at 11:32 PM

Kobe fronts on trying to be like Mike

Kobe is the latest to be the called "The Next Jordan" (following Grant Hill, Penny Hardaway, and ahem... Harold "Baby Jordań" Miner(?)), but he is also the closest to backing up the talk, on the court that is. Though Kobe falls short in charisma, and the making his teammates better department, in an interview recently with ESPN's Stephen A. Smith, the analyst alluded to the comparisons and Kobe acted like he was tired of hearing it. "Let me do me" is what the Lower Marion High School phenom was saying.

Kobe please....

I for one don't buy it. Kobe wants to be Mike so bad he may have an accident in his pants.

Let's break it down:

1) Kobe early in his career while driving the lane would stick his tongue out, a Jordan signature.

166

2) Kobe famously, or infamously, waved off Karl Malone in an All-Star Game when he saw Jordan was guarding him, prompting Malone to go on a these-young-whippersnappers-don't-have-any-respect-for-the-game tirades after the game. I thought Karl was gonna put Kobe over his knee.

3) Speaking of Utah, Kobe chose to take multiple questionable three pointers in a playoff game in 1997 with the last being an airball in an attempt to win the game all by himself, another Jordan staple.

4) Kobe changed his jersey from #8 to #24. Ofcourse Michael Jordan wore #23 so Kobe wearing #24 means Kobe is one up on Jordan, making him better (this is purely speculation on my part)

5) In the Kobe Olympic commercials Bryant is wearing the number 27. Michael Jordan's number on the Dream Team in 1992 was 9. 27... 2 + 7 = 9. Kobe's official Olympic jersey number is 10. Again 10 is one more than 9. You do the math... (this is purely speculation on my part, but with Kobe's ego, it makes a whole lot of sense).

Stop frontin' Kobe!

Just my thoughts...

Posted by Jamiyl Samuels at 11:40 PM

Wednesday June 25, 2008

I think I figured something out about Imus...

...he ain't too bright. Why in the hell in da hell would he even... after what happened in April of last year, April 12th to be exact is when he got canned, I was at the station where he worked when it happened answering a lot of calls from angry white people who couldn't believe people made a big deal of Imus calling a bunch of young black women who are in college playing organized sports "nappy-headed hoes".

Anyway, after the huge firestorm, why would you even mention about somebody's color?

For those who don't know what happened, Warner Wolf told Imus that Adam "Pacman" Jones, the former Tennessee Titans and current Dallas Cowboys cornerback had been arrested six times since he has been drafted in 2005. This brain surgeon (Imus) asks Wolf "what color is he?". Who was working the boards in that studio? Not someone with Imus' or ABC radio's best interest in mind. Hit the "dump" button, man! Don't let the comment air.

It makes no sense to me. Where a black man probably wouldn't have been given another opportunity to have a talk show, this rocket scientist (Imus), after just a couple months of being back on air goes on to put hmself in the position where his words can be taken out of context. He knows there are African-American watchdogs sitting by the radio like Cedric the Entertainer in Kings Of Comedy " I wish a mutha***** would...."

...and he did. Maybe he's senile.

I can't call it. These folks keep Al Sharpton in business. They complain that they can't stand him, yet they continue to do dumb s*** which brings him back out in front of the cameras.

But I digress...

Posted by Jamiyl Samuels at 12:05 AM

Saturday June 28, 2008

Where Are The Female Emcees?

Below is a story I wrote on the lack of
female emcees in Hip Hop back in
February of 2007 that was published on
a major New York radio station's
website. Within months, magazines and
Hip Hop sites were asking the same
question selling magazines and ad space
behind it. A coincidence or lazy
journalism? I say it's the latter.
While I can say I am not the first to
touch on this topic, a lot more people
started asking the question all of a
sudden. Just my thoughts... but I
digress.

Shout out to Victoria Fleary for the
exposure early and BET for holding a
town hall meeting on the subject.

Where are the Female Emcees?
Words by Jamiyl Samuels

*Remember when Roxanne Shante was going at
UTFO? Who was this little girl capitalizing off of a
fictitious object of desire for Kangol Kid, Doctor Ice,*

and Educated Rapper? One thing for sure, Shante had guts. She also had a future legend co-signing her in Marley Marl, helpful in the male-dominated sport such as Hip Hop. Remember Sha Rock of Funky Four Plus One? Salt N' Pepa's venomous retort to the classic Doug E. Fresh and Slick Rick anthem "The Show"? Who could forget Monie Love's cameo on Queen Latifah's ode to female empowerment "Ladies First", a spot that ultimately led to her own solo shot ("Monie In the Middle", anyone?). Everyone knows MC Lyte, or at least, should know. Who else brought us the classic "10% Dis" with the classic "Hot damn hoe here we go again" jab, "Paper Thin" and "Ruffneck", a song which redefined a woman's preference in men at that time?

If you are of the 106 and Park set, too young to remember these female pioneers, take a listen to Nas' "Where Are They Now?" ('cuz nowadays "old school artists" are never relevant until a respected current artist shouts them out) then google accordingly. Female emcees, also known as "femcees", have made an indelible mark on the culture since the early days. Repeatedly written off as a novelty act, they continue to persevere through the hate, stereotype and doubt of their peers. It is this lack of proverbial respect which has birthed some of the most fascinating music from these women.

As Hip Hop lost its inhibitions and became big business in the mid-nineties the next generation of lady microphone slayers ushered in a sexual revolution. Foxy Brown, Lil' Kim, and Eve spearheaded this movement, viewed by many as a gimmick. One thing for sure, you never heard women spit like those three spit. They spoke of their sexual prowess and it was empowering. As rappers liberally used the word "bitch", women would embrace the word as their own. They would flaunt the bodies that were being repeatedly objectified by their male counterparts with mediocre rhyme skill. They were the video model with rhymes galore. They were so good in fact it was assumed someone had to be writing their rhymes. B.I.G. was writing all of Kim's rhymes, Jay-Z was writing Foxy's stuff, but who was writing for Eve? DMX? You had to give these women credit. They had something to say in the 80's and the 90's.

Remember when Foxy and Kim were the "Thelma and Louise" of Hip Hop? When Eve was "the vicious pit bull in a skirt", showing off the seductive paw print tattoos on her chest? Fast forward to the new millennium, Foxy is reportedly hitting manicurists with cell phones, Lil' Kim was thrown in jail for perjury, wrote songs about it, we wanted to hear it, "hear" it go… brick. Eve has been signed to

Aftermath since 1990 (ok…maybe not that long, but you get the idea) and has yet to release an album. Her tattoos mysteriously airbrushed for FCC approval on her self-titled sitcom. Who will fill the void? Trina? Jacki-O? Khia? Again, who will fill the void? Is this what the female rap game has come to? Listening to the aforementioned pugilists fight for "Queen of the South"? You can't go out like this, ladies. We gotta embrace Jean Grae. Embrace Remy Ma, both of whom put out good music that has flown under the radar due to lack of promotion.

Maybe karma is saying something different. Foxy was set to release her long awaited album, her first since reuniting with Jay-Z, then… bam… she went deaf…literally. You can't make that up. Kim was set to drop "The Naked Truth" then… bam… locked up like Akon and Styles. The album, a stellar piece of lyrical dexterity and sonic wizadry, falls by the wayside due to Kim's inaccessibility. And Eve has been on Aftermath since… oh we already established that.

For now, I am still anticipating Foxy's "Black Roses", despite the awkward press conferences in churches in loud green tops with matching eyeliner. I am rooting for Lil' Kim to regain motivation on this tenth anniversary of Biggie's death and recapture the magic of "Hardcore". I am pulling for Eve to just come out period, she of the "Chronic" size delay between albums. I urge you young'uns not to turn your back on the foremothers. We need a little history to give the future a kick in the behind. We can't bring back the fall of '96 or the summer of '89, but as long as they are alive and the fire is in them, female emcees can still make an impact. There is currently a woman with a legitimate shot at being the next president of the United States, so the possibilities are endless for women more so than ever. Now is not the time to disappear.

To update, Eve still hasn't come out, Foxy tried to do her own version of jailhouse rap and blamed the label for her failure (she's since run into the arms of Rick Ross and is talking marriage - is it that bad, Foxy?), Lil' Kim is doing cameos, but her future is still uncertain, Remy Ma got gangsta and tried to merck her best friend over a few dollars and is serving time, and Eve still hasn't come out with... Lauryn Hill is still having babies and looking straight out of the Universoul Circus, and Eve...

I mean, just look at who was up for a BET Award for best female emcee this past week: Kid Sister? Trina? Really?

MC Lyte is holding y'all up right now ladies (my apologies to the underground femme fatales). Stay out of jail and let's take it back to '89 or '96 dammit. Hell, I'll take 2001.

Posted by Jamiyl Samuels at 4:29 PM

Wednesday August 29, 2008

Yes We Can...

On the night of August 28th 2008 history was made on a historic night. On the 45th anniversary of Dr. Martin Luther King's "I Have A Dream" speech, Illinois senator Barack Obama became the first African-American to be named the candidate of a major political party by accepting the Presidential nomination for the Democratic Party. Obama appeared in front of a crowd of over 80,000 delegates, super delegates and supporters (some Hillary converts) to let them all know why he is the right choice to lead America.

In 45 riveting minutes, Obama laid

out his plan for a better America
with the verve, poise, and urgency of
a 34 year old Martin Luther King so
many years ago. As Obama eloquently
put it, Dr. King could have addressed
the audience that day with a message
of despair, negativity about the
segregation and racial division that
ravaged America, particularly the
South. Instead Dr. King chose to
speak of hope for a better tomorrow,
the same way Obama spoke of a nation
that is "better than the last eight
years".

It was fitting that Obama made
history 45 years after a historic
address at the feet of a statue of
Abraham Lincoln, another visionary.
If Dr. King, even Coretta Scott King,
were alive today I am sure his eyes
would have welled up, as did so many
in the crowd last night including
Oprah Winfrey, with tears at the
significance of the moment. Even if
Obama loses in November, to make it
this far shows how far African-
Americans have come in a country
where Blacks could not even go to the
same schools, use the same bathrooms,
sit in the same seat as Caucasian

people. As I watched Obama's speech as CNN's cameras scanned the crowd, there were Caucasians, Latinos, Asians, Native Americans, and African-Americans standing side by side in some places, all riveted, hanging on every word, believing that Obama, an African-American male, is the right person to lead their country.

Now that it is official, I leave this post with an e-mail I received. For all the hope and optimism of the Democratic National Convention, Barack Obama is still an African-American in politics with a very real chance of being President of the United States of America. In a country that has seen the assassination of the aforementioned Abraham Lincoln, John F. Kennedy, and Democratic Presidential nominee Robert Kennedy, all men who tried to assist in the integration of African-Americans. With that said, I leave you with this:

Dear God, I pray for optimum health, wisdom, mental clarity and political prosperity for Barack Obama, and for his **protection**, as he seeks to become our President! Amen.

Posted by Jamiyl Samuels at 10:41 AM

Sunday August 31, 2008

Thirty Something

I will be 30 years old on September 1st. A milestone no doubt as many young black men and women never make it to 30 much less their 25th birthday. You can include The Notorious B.I.G, Tupac Shakur, and most recently Heath Ledger as some of the more famous people cut down before they celebrated a third decade on Earth.

For those of us who are fortunate enough to hit 30, the question should be asked: Are you satisfied with your life? It is a double ended question because in reality one should never be satisfied as there is always more to learn and strive for. At 30 you are five years removed from a quarter of your life. 30 begins a new chapter: not necessarily middle age, but a time where your life needs to be put in perspective. If you are not where you think you should be, don't blame

society, or the government, or family.
Take control of your destiny and make
it happen!

Pursue your dream whether it be going
to and completing college, getting
married to the love of your life,
becoming a doctor or police officer,
making the NBA, NFL, Major Leagues or
buying a home.

People will tell you what you should do
with your life or stunt your growth.
While looking out for others is an
admirable quality, don't forget to do
you or you may miss out on the
satisfaction of realizing your dream.

For me, 30 is not the new 20, but a new
start. A clean slate to accomplish what
I didn't in my 20's. To amend for the
time I feel I wasted pursuing a career
that I probably wasn't ready for. The
fact that I may live to see the first
Black President of the United States is
special, now can I channel the work
ethic to achieve my goals as Barack
Obama has to reach where he is, that is
the 30 million dollar question. If I
can, my friends, not only will I be a
best-selling author, I will be a
blockbuster screenwriter and filmmaker

as well as a Grammy winner for the accompanying soundtrack....

Keep Your Eyes Open for me...

God Bless

Posted by Jamiyl Samuels at 10:13 PM

Thursday September 11, 2008

LL COOL J "Exit 13"

It is not my intention to do CD reviews on my blog (that is for a future outlet), but I had to comment on the latest CD from Hip Hop legend LL Cool J (I know it runs a little long, but the great thing about a blog is I am not confined to a word count, but will be happy to do a revised version - I am a freelancer).

LL Cool J - "Exit 13" (Def Jam) **rating**
**** *out of* *********

By now it should be common knowledge that it is not wise to count out LL Cool J. Still even as his physical appearance has continued to defy the harsh realities of middle age, his place in today's assembly line rap

scene has come into question...again.
Students of the true school have seen
this movie before.

One need look no further than the year
1989 when "The Future of the Funk" was
roundly criticized by his peers for the
abundance of materialism in his rhymes.
Where he can be now credited for
incredible foresight, the lukewarm
reception to *"Walking With A
Panther"* set the stage for Uncle L's
magnum opus 1990's *"Mama Said Knock You
Out"*. L tells the media "don't call it
a comeback" as he indeed attacks the
microphone with the ferocity of his
earlier albums while offering scathing
responses to his detractors on the
title track and "Eat Em' Up L (Chill)".

One can also recall a young
whippersnapper named Canibus, who in
1997 felt LL had lost enough
credibility in the streets ("99 percent
of your fans wear high heels") that he
could take on the pride of Farmer's
Boulevard. LL not only won the battle
with Canibus, but returned proclaiming
to be The Greatest Of All Time
(*G.O.A.T*) in 2000, an album sporting
one radio/video single ("Imagine That")
and a bunch of street-oriented material

that proved L was still hard as hell.

Fast forward to 2008. Disgruntled with the promotional efforts behind his 12th album *Todd* Smith and the direction of Def Jam under labelmate Jay-Z, LL proclaimed his 13th album would be his last under the house that Rick (Rubin) and Russ(ell Simmons) built, thus the title of the album. L minced no words when voicing his displeasure about the then-president Carter stirring speculation of another Jay-Z/Nas type of battle between legends. The battle never happened, but L aligned himself with 50 Cent, a man known to save a career or two. With the odds firmly stacked against him once more, LL responded like the free agent he is.

On *Exit 13* performs like CC Sabathia after the trade to Milwaukee. The first thing that jumps out at the listener is the strain in LL's voice as the soaring opening track "It's Time For War" booms. The familiar tone that graced classics like "Radio" and "I'm Bad" resonates here and on "You Better Watch Me" where a rejuvenated Uncle L bellows "oh you wanna take it to the '90's?".

LL is indeed at his best when he melds

the true school and the new school as witnessed in his choice of production (Marley Marl, the architect of "Mama Said", returns to produce two joints), and features. The winner here is the Grandmaster Caz featured "This Is Ringtone Murder", a stab at the plethora of rappers selling a hit single as a cell phone accessory while lacking the substance needed to sustain an entire album, where the Ripper returns with daggers like: "sounding like girls with your sweet sixteen...test big Elly come get your head sprung...". The highly-anticipated G-Unit union never materializes as 50 Cent only appears on the hook of the possible follow-up single "Can You Feel My Heartbeat". "Cry" is a send-up of the 2001 Ja Rule/Lil' Mo duet "I Cry" whose driving production and superior crooning from Lil' Mo could land a few radio spins.

The first half of the album is pleasantly surprising for the aforementioned reasons, however, as if Cool J feels he has proven his point to the naysayers, the album loses considerable steam after "Ringtone Murder". From the cheesy Bollywood soundtrack of "I Fall In Love" and predictable patriotic production of "American Girl", the filler material comes in bunches. L's final salvo is worthy as "Dear Hip Hop" is one of the better Hip Hop as a person tunes.

While 19 tracks prove to be too many for the G.O.A.T to handle, Todd Smith proves on the rap superhighway he doesn't need AAA (or AARP for that matter) and an early exit would be premature.

Posted by Jamiyl Samuels at 9:46 PM

Friday October 10, 2008

Keep the Faith - Book review

I just finished reading recording artist Faith Evans' memoir *"Keep The Faith"* yesterday. Best known for being the "first lady" signed to Sean "Puffy" Combs' Bad Boy Records and subsequently releasing top-selling albums with titles featuring her name, Faith collaborates with well-known scribe Aliya S. King to document her rise from small-time New Jersey choir girl to the top of the R&B charts and all the drama in between. Most of the drama revolves around her first husband, fellow music

superstar Christopher "Notorious
B.I.G." Wallace.

This book is an excellent read simply
because Faith makes up her mind to take
the reader through a tour of her
pianful and private past sugarcoating
nothing. Although it has been over 11
years since The Notorious B.I.G.
tragically lost his life, Faith
resurrects the big man through numerous
anecdotes of their turbulent marriage
giving the reader insight into events
that transpired behind the scenes
during various infamous occurrences
(i.e. Tupac's initial shooting in 1994,
Faith's meeting with Tupac, her battles
with Lil' Kim, etc.).

Faith humanizes herself in her memoir
by not making any excuses for her
behavior including her propensity to
fall in love hard and fast with the
wrong people (i.e. a married man, which
she rationalizes is a sin and will
bring bad karma in her future). The
characters in the book, especially the
ones not in the spotlight, are vividly
brought to life (her mom, her pseudo-
grandparents, her friends from New
Jersey) allowing the reader to follow
along seamlessly.

I remember being in high school when the East Coast/West Coast controversy was happening, including watching The Source Awards, with the only way to follow was through media speculation in magazines, radio, and music. *"Keep The Faith"* gives a bird's eye view of the conflict from Evans who was thrust into the heart of the it. The inner turmoil she faced from being the object of public ridicule is very revealing. Great tidbits like Redman (Reggie) being Faith's first boyfriend, to being given her early start by R&B stars Christopher Williams and Al B. Sure, to Notorious B.I.G's tearful apology for putting the "2 Pacs" line in "Brooklyn's Finest", this memoir does not disappoint.

A bit repeptitive and out of sequence (i.e. her NBA lover says he's in L.A. for All-Star Weekend, usually in February, yet she meets Tupac in the same scene just released from prison and goes to the soundtrack release for "Waiting to Exhale" - a late 1995 release.)in some places, but a minor transgression. With the sacrifices Faith has made and the enormous amount of drama she goes through, the aptly titled *"Keep The Faith"* is a testament to the strong black and gifted woman Faith Evans is.

Friday November 7, 2008

Did You Vote?

Somewhere Dr. Martin Luther King, Jr. is smiling as confirmation of his fight for equal rights for all races, ethnicities, and creeds, immortalized in his "I Have A Dream Speech" 40 years ago, materializes in the election of the first African-American President of the United States of America: Barack Obama. Obama is proof that a Black Man can be anything he wants to be, not just a rapper or athlete. His wife Michelle Obama, a decorated law professional with multiple degrees is proof that Black women are just as essential to the success of Black men, and that there are no limits to what they can achieve, something Condoleeza Rice has proven over the last eight years.

As I stood in line to cast my vote this past Tuesday, I, like many others, was impressed by the outpouring of minorities young and old, able and disabled, who wanted to be a part of history. I was especially touched by the young children who consistently demanded that they get a chance to vote to their parents.

I want to thank all the White people who voted for Obama. Your actions have shown that we as a country can look past race in favor of a candidate who represents a change for all people.

None need look any further than Obama's acceptance speech. Where a candidate would be smiling from ear to ear basking in the historical moment, Obama exuded calm in the midst of the euphoria. He was a man not satisfied with becoming President-elect, but with letting his constituents know the task ahead is a formidable one.

It was a speech that recalled the genesis of his journey from Presidential candidate, carefully recognizing the people from all walks of life that made his campaign run possible with selfless donations, to the monumental night on November 4th 2008. He thanked John McCain (whose concession speech was just as poignant and powerful) and Sarah Palin, his campaign managers and his family. He even reached out to the people who did not vote for him (who does that in an acceptance speech, I ask you?). World leaders and civilians rejoiced at the choice made by the United States, thrusting our nation again to the forefront of innovators and foward thinkers in the eyes of the World, hopefully going a long way to heal any global animosity festering from the last eight years.

Even in victory Obama never wavered from his message, realistically stating that he could not cure all the nation's ills in one year or one term, but he would be honest with the American people. After an unpopular war started on suspect intelligence and alleged government corruption, all we ask for is honesty from our President.

Congratulations Barack Obama, the real work begins now. The same rules apply for an African-American in the workforce: you have to work twice as hard as the next, watch your back, and be safe.

That's all...

Incidentally, were you able to get a
newspaper on the morning of November
5th?
Please let me know in the poll.

Thanks,

Sunday November 16, 2008

The Roots

I love The Roots, the legendary Hip Hop
band out of Philadelphia. in fact, they
are my favorite Hip Hop group, next to
A Tribe Called Quest (support the new
Q-Tip album *The Renaissance*)who
technically aren't together at the
moment so that would make The Roots my
favorite group, but I digress.

I watch a lot of Noggin because of my
20-month old son (notice how I blame my
son for this guilty pleasure of mine).
I saw a recent episode of "Yo Gabba
Gabba" and who should I see during a
musical interlude, but "The Legendary"
ones themselves. Black Thought wasn't
spitting fire this time, oh no.

190

Guitarist "Captain Kirk", rarely used vocally, displayed his superior singing talent in a song about family. It was great to see the entire band on the colorful set (Kamal grooving on keys, Questlove on the drums and Black Thought with the hilarious vocal accompaniment) having fun and sending a message to kids.

Seeing The Roots gave "Yo Gabba Gabba" a little more credibility in my eyes (even though I was already converted, a far cry from when I first saw the title and angrily changed the channel in disgust at what I thought was another exploitation of Hip Hop culture by way of suspect Hip Hop vernacular). I thought the title and the buffonish looking lead "DJ Lance" was a disgraceful stereotype of young Black males and Hip Hop culture not fit for kids to study. However, I changed my tune when forced to watch the program over time (I can't monitor my son's cartoons from work) and saw that the themes ranging from being polite to others, family, to what to do with a loose tooth, were valuable lessons that were more important than the physical appearance of the host. With guest spots from R&B recording artist Mya, rapper Biz Markie, and Pheonix Suns star Amare Stoudamire teaching kids dance steps, dribbling moves, beatboxing and more, the show isn't half bad.

Shout out to The Roots for diversifying their musical portfolio. They need to give "Kirk" more shine on future recordings (sidebar: doesn't Scott Storch -the predecessor of Kamal on the keys- wish he stayed with the group now?).

Just my thoughts...

Yo Gabba.... lol.

Hip Hop forever...

That's all

Posted by Jamiyl Samuels at 2:28 PM

Friday March 20, 2009

Back for '09

Happy New Year, and good riddance to Winter (even though Spring came in with a nice snow storm in New York). I am

back from my "blog-atus" or blog
hiatus. A lot of things have happened
so far this year, the most obvious
being the "Chrihanna" situation (who
started blending celebrity names
anyway? Horrible move).

My take on abusive relationships is
this, no man should hit a woman for any
reason. A female can hit a man only if
she caught him doing something that
could jeopardize her emotional and
physical health (cheating with another
woman or, even worse, another man -
then she could kill him... j/k).
Otherwise, ladies should keep their
hands to themselves. If you have to
consistently hit your man, you need to
leave the situation because it is
unhealthy. Good for Rihanna for finally
leaving Chris.

Chris is 19! He has a lot of nerve
beating on any female at his age. Sure
he saw domestic violence growing up,
but, think about it... he allegedly
beat up Rihanna because she got mad at
him for getting an alleged booty call
from someone he was sleeping with
during their relationship.

I would feel a little sympathy for him

if photos didn't come out of him jet
skiing and smiling in Miami. A little
remorse? Just a smidgen? Please?

Rihanna has split, for now. Some women
don't get a chance to walk away.

Now on another topic:

I thought Barack Obama was hilarious on
The Tonight Show on Thursday night. I
thought at the moment he made the
Special Olympics comment in reference
to his bowling was not malicious in
intent. Upon further review I can see
where the Special Olympics people would
be up in arms, but NO ONE ELSE.

Come On! The "uproar" over this screams
watchdog group.

It was like Republicans and Obama
detractors were glued to the television
waiting for something they can
criticize. Lord knows they got on him
for filling out an NCAA bracket on
Sportscenter. The man is a human being.
Must everything he does be political?
Plenty of Republican Congressman have
shown they use plenty of leisure time
in bathroom stalls, with Pages, and
women not their wife, etc. Can Obama

194

have an interest in sports and focus on the economy at the same time?

I guess not.

Just my thoughts ladies and gentlemen...

Posted by Jamiyl Samuels at 2:42 PM

Wednesday January 13, 2010

Steroid "King" Comes Clean

One of the early sports shockers (or not) of 2010 is the admission by former Major League Baseball slugger Mark McGwire that he used performance enhancing drugs during the height of his career (including the 1998 season). For avid sports fans this has been the worst kept secret in all of sports (the best kept secret being Andre Agassi using crystal meth before his tennis matches, but I digress).

Many remember the infamous "I am not here to talk about the past" comment (or lack thereof) he repeatedly threw at Congress in 2005. Many more remember the fantastic, aforementioned, summer of 1998 when McGwire and Chicago Cubs "slugger" (and fellow steroid suspect) Sammy Sosa singlehandedly took baseball off of life support after the crippling strike of 1994 with a mythic display of homerun power that ultimately led to both men crushing the previous single season homerun record held by Roger Maris.

That year McGwire hit 70 (!) homeruns and Sosa 66 (!!). I admit I, like the rest of the nation, got caught up in the magic not giving a second thought that I was watching chemically enhanced power. It had been a few years since the league became dominated by the long ball, replete with the "chicks dig the long ball" commercials from Nike including Greg Maddux and Tom Glavine two of the greatest pitchers of all time.

In hindsight I am kicking myself for not sensing something was amiss when Brady Anderson of the Baltimore Orioles suddenly hits 50 homeruns from the leadoff spot in 1996, Todd Hundley, while playing catcher for the New York Mets crushes over 40 homeruns in the same year (while former Met Darryl Strawberry - the definitive slugger of his generation - barely hit 40 homeruns at the height of his powers in the 80's).

McGwire was the story of that 1998 season and he soared in popularity playing the reluctant superstar/savior. What a fraud. McGwire, ready to return to baseball as a (*stifling laughter*)*hitting coach* for the St. Louis Cardinals, finally decides to confirm what was confirmed five years ago in front of Congress. He says he called the widow of Roger Maris to apologize. I mean the gall of this guy is amazing.

There is McGwire, after breaking a homerun record that Maris went through hell to set (breaking the record of the almighty Babe Ruth), hugging Maris' wife and sons in the front row of Busch Stadium after hitting number 62. There are Maris' boys (a spitting image of their father) crying on McGwire's massive steroid injected shoulders overcome with emotion. I'd be crying to, with anger. How could McGwire in good conscience put on such a farce?

I can with great conviction say McGwire ruined baseball that season. Not only did he break a longstanding homerun record illegally, he made homeruns the only thing that mattered in baseball validating use by players who might have been on the fence (not only will you be the star of your team, but you will get a bunch of money as well), he arguably provoked the current all-time homerun "leader" Barry Bonds to get on the sauce (reportedly jealous at all the attention McGwire was getting Bonds started juicing to steal the spotlight away from McGwire) when he already had a Hall of Fame career locked up, and caused Jose Canseco to blow the whistle on the culture he allegedly made famous in a book that exposed players, coaches, media and the Commissioner's ineptitude in preventing widespread steroid use.

Well done, Mark.

Now we have to hear how sorry you are. We have to see tears of a real clown, crying because he got caught. The real travesty, if there could be one greater, is the response of McGwire's coach Tony LaRussa. LaRussa, McGwire's coach in Oakland and St. Louis repeatedly insulted the media's and fans intelligence by defending McGwire's "workout regimen" and

character. When McGwire admitted his
use, LaRussa claimed he found out the
same time the rest of the world did.
Two days ago. Please.

LaRussa continues to be a McGwire
apologist, applauding him for coming
clean and not "blatingly" using the
drugs to cheat, but to heal his body.
And I got the Brooklyn and Manhattan
bridges in my house for sale. Any other
coach would be appalled at the
revelation, if they were truly shocked
by it, and given McGwire the heave-ho
from any staff position. Not LaRussa.
Makes me wanna throw up.

LaRussa defending McGwire sends just as
bad a message to kids as McGwire using
and setting records artificially. That
McGwire can just retire, fade into
obscurity for most of the 2000's and
just come out of the woodwork and land
a high profile position on one of the
more high profile teams in Major League
Baseball teaches kids nothing, but if
you cheat you can lay low come back and
still succeed in life.

Well done, Tony.

I mean really, what kind of credibility

does McGwire have as a hitting coach anyway? I wouldn't take him seriously? This guy had tons of media surrounding the batting cage filming his batting practice like it was a postgame press conference. We know now officially that those "majestic" shots were artificially enhanced. What a letdown. It hurt me enough that I had to hear A-Rod, who was the last hope to break the homerun record legally, admit to steroid use, Manny Ramirez is now linked to steroid use, who is left? Albert Pujols? Ken Griffey Jr.? Instead of embracing Pujols you are left waiting for when that story will come that exposes Pujols as another cheat. How can you enjoy baseball when you're thinking like that?

I mean, the Mets of the 80's did drugs, but their homeruns were clean even if their urine wasn't. That's the baseball I remember growing up. I thought it came back in 1998, but I was dead wrong.

Can we give Jose Canseco his props already? And why would McGwire continue to deny anything Canseco says now? As we have found out Canseco told the truth when he had nothing to lose. Now

Canseco is challenging McGwire to a public lie detector test. Canseco is not going to go away. He is a publicity whore who is giving the finger to baseball each time his name is mentioned in connection with these idiot ballplayers who continue to cheat the system and cry about trying to heal their body when they get caught. Canseco is like a bully. McGwire chose to return to the public eye and he needs to tell the whole truth.

Take the power away from Canseco. No one has been able to do that to this point.

Just my thoughts ladies and gentlemen...

Posted by Jamiyl Samuels at 10:20 AM

Tuesday June 29, 2010

Chris Breezy Breaks down

I did not see Chris Brown's performance at the 2010 BET Awards live, but I did catch the broadcast of the afterparty and heard everyone talking about how Chris tore it down. Just hearing Chris Brown's name and the BET awards in the same sentence was shocking enough seeing that they all but banned him from the building in 2009, days after Michael Jackson died. I have had the pleasure in the past of personally seeing Chris Brown channel Michael Jackson and I was floored at how effortlessly he did Michael's moves, so to have a Michael Jackson tribute last year without Chris did not feel right. I understand why BET could not have Brown perform with wounds from his assault on Rihanna still raw in people's minds.

After seeing a short highlight of Brown's performance I had to find it on YouTube. Everyone is making a big deal about him crying on stage saying he wasn't sincere, he was looking for sympathy, yada yada yada. "Man In the Mirror" is a powerful song in its call for people to look within themselves and make a change for the better before helping others in need. The irony of the song and the significance it has in Brown's own life at this point - of course the guy is going to break down. That does not mean he is looking for sympathy in my opinion.

I am positive he is genuinely sorry he

laid hands on Rihanna and he misses Michael Jackson. I haven't seen anyone do Michael's moves spot on like that since a young Alfonso Ribeiro (Carlton from Fresh Prince of Bel-Air to the youths) in the 1984 Pepsi commercial. A young guy who studies Michael Jackson like that and incorporates his dances into all performances has a definite love for MJ that would cause a break down such as we saw.

I believe Chris. As I said before "Man In the Mirror" is a powerful song from an otherworldly talented singer/songwriter/performer/humanitaria n that tugs on the heartstrings and conscience of people who take their good fortune (not only monetary, but health as well) for granted. I think it is time to forgive this young man for his horrible lapse in judgment. While I do not condone his actions in the slightest bit, he has plead guilty, he is serving his time with community service, and he has been blackballed in the music industry. Bravo to BET for giving Brown the cathartic experience of paying tribute to his idol. After criticizing last year's tribute and funeral from the peanut gallery, Chris got his chance to do his thing where he

is most comfortable... the stage. Sound
familiar?

Tuesday August 31, 2010

Nicki is a Monster

Just heard that new Kanye joint
"Monster". Nicki Minaj is a problem
with a capital "P". I haven't stopped
what I was doing to listen to a verse
in a long time. I have to admit Nicki's
voices are very entertaining and make
her stand out not just amongst women,
but the guys as well. Anyone on a track
with Jay-Z that rhymes after him (even
though he has rhymed first or seond on
a few memorable super posse cuts -
i.e. "It's Murder" by the defunct
"Murder Inc." of he, DMX and Ja Rule,
and "Swagga Like Us") has got something
special. Next thing you know she will
be rhyming after Busta Rhymes on a
posse cut.

She might be bigger than Drake when her
album drops in November.

It kinda feels good to say that about a
female MC. With Lauryn Hill reportedly

getting back to her "Miseducation" swag and Lil' Kim reportedly signing to Roc Nation, and Foxy Brown ready to break out with new music, the femcee could be back in effect.

Posted by Jamiyl Samuels at 1:20 AM

Note: I begin to realize I can add pictures to spice up my blog. Who knew?

Tuesday October 5, 2010

Five reasons the Miami Heat will NOT win the NBA title this year

5 - Erik Spoelstra is coach

Let's be honest here. Pat Riley (and all the slick hair, championship pedigree, and Showtime glory that comes with him) is the reason LeBron James took his talents to South Beach. The last time the Heat won the title in 2006, Pat Riley was on the sidelines and a still serviceable Shaquille O'Neal (another Riley signing) was in the pivot. If you remember once Shaq signed in 2004, Riley "Deebo'ed" the coaching reins from another assistant turned coach Stan Van Gundy. Erik Spoelstra took over the job once Shaq rolled out of town and the team became a joke again. Even though everyone is saying the right things in defense of the current head coach, you better believe if this super team with the plethora of nicknames gets off to a slow start (read: three game losing streak) expect to see Riles back on the sidelines in a hurry.

4 – Chemistry

Although it is a given that whenever players are put together for the first time there will be an adjustment period, these aren't just any players. The "New Big Three" of LeBron James, Dwyane Wade and Chris Bosh are not only three of the top ten players in the league they were also, in Bosh and James' case, the superstar of their old teams. These three are used to having the ball in their hands. Add to that the twelve other makeshift players they threw the roster together with and it may take some time to get the ball rolling.

3 - Pressure

The fallout from LeBron's "Decision" has been swift. His good guy image took a significant hit for the way he left Cleveland and teaming up with Dwyane Wade and Chris Bosh means anything less than an appearance in the NBA Finals would be a disappointment. With former NBA coach and ESPN/ABC analyst Jeff Van Gundy stating on record that this team will surpass the 72 win season of the 1995-96 Chicago Bulls, to say expectations are high would be an understatement.

2 - The Other NBA Teams

Forget about the other teams that were left at the altar by LeBron James (Knicks, Nets, Bulls, Clippers, and Cavaliers) Orlando Magic center Dwight Howard has already publicly disparaged the "other" Florida NBA team in the press as overhyped. With the Miami Heat already being given the NBA title by many before the season starts, the other 385 NBA players are not happy with the notion that they are suiting up to lose. Therefore expect every team that plays the Heat this season to play their best game in hopes of derailing the South Beach juggernaut. And that is just the regular season. The playoffs are another animal entirely.

1 - Kobe

His team won the NBA championship last
season and his focus is on a repeat
three peat, a feat that would equal his
idol Michael Jordan. Expecting a
showdown with LeBron's Cavs the last
two seasons, Kobe will not just hand
the title over to the Heat without a
fight. Like Jordan, Kobe thrives off
challenges and all the hype surrounding
"Miami Thrice" will only fuel his fire.

Posted by Jamiyl Samuels at 2:11 PM

Tuesday June 7, 2011

Weiner Confesses

The punchlines couldn't be laid out any
easier for late-night talk show hosts
and comedians around the country. With
a last name that is synonymous
with sausage, Rep. Anthony Weiner
should know better than to get caught
with his shirt off and his pants down
sexting via social media. He should
know that there are watchdogs hiding in
the cyber bushes waiting for our
congressmen, governors, and President
to slip up so they can fan the flames
of scandal.

Yet these idiots continue to get caught
in a compromising position. They
continue to vehemently deny the

accusatory questions only to tearfully admit their indiscretions, with the humiliated spouse as the innocent bystander.

There was Governor Eliot Spitzer, champion of all things moral and ethical in his fight to rid the streets of scum only to be exposed as a connoisseur of fine smut. How he landed back on television I do not know. There was "Ahnold the Governator" Schwarzenegger, poster man for every gratuitously bloody action-hero stereotype (which he was never criticized yet Black movies set in urban neighborhoods with the same violence were derided as negative for kids) somehow got voted into public office we now know three or four years AFTER fathering a bastard son with his housekeeper. These are dirty secrets that are supposed to be unearthed BEFORE the politician makes it into office, right? Exactly who was in charge of the vetting process here? Bad enough his wife Maria Shriver had the unfortunate ties to the Kennedy clan and all their alleged history of philandering, she has to deal with this demoralizing betrayal from a man who most surely now groped those

women that accused him during
his campaign.

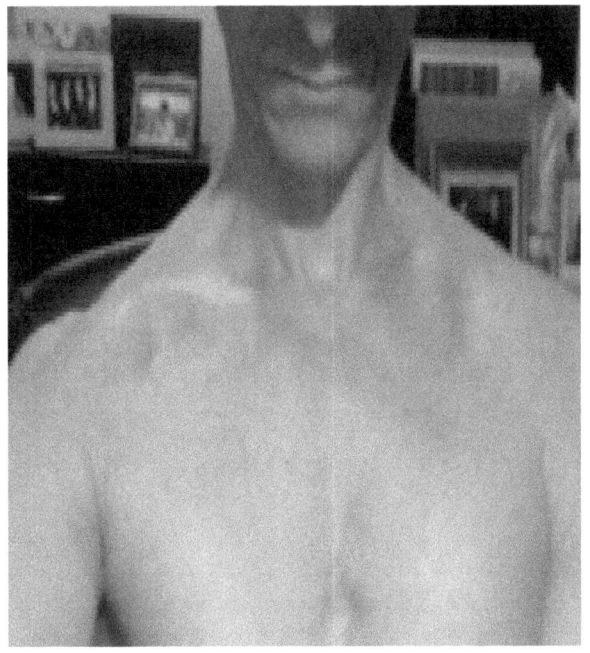

And here we have Mr. Tater Tot, er...
Weiner. He of the passionate rant on
the House floor months ago, will now be
known for posting lewd pictures on
Twitter. For following a porn star on
Twitter. Things that have nothing to do
with his political acumen, but will
bring him down nonetheless.

You know the NBA has a symposium for
incoming rookies letting them know

about the perils and pitfalls and, more importantly, the great responsibility they are taking on to not only conduct themselves with integrity, dignity and respect, but to also respect that they are the face of their employer: the NBA. They screw up, the NBA as a whole looks bad.

Maybe politicians need something like this to remind them that they are the face of the constituents they say they are fighting for. These repeated indiscretions destroy all confidence and credibility, sorta like that guy who predicted the end of the world would come two weeks ago. His followers are still trying to re-establish a presence in society, like they just came out of jail or something.

Ridiculous.

How do these guys allow the stupidest things to derail them is beyond me.

Obama, you better not....

That's all I'm gonna say...

Posted by Jamiyl Samuels at 6:55 AM

212

Saturday September 10, 2011

9/11: 10 Years Later

It's crazy to think 10 years have
passed since the most deadliest attack
on U.S. soil. Still I remember where I
was, what I was doing, where I was
going and how I eventually got home on
that Tuesday. I was supposed to be off

from work at The Wiz Electronics store
that day and I switched with another
co-worker. I worked in Brooklyn, but I
had to go to another store in Queens to
help clean up. The day was like any
other, the sun was out, not a cloud in
the sky. I took the train to Queens and
when the train emerged from the
underground tunnel outdoors I noticed
people on the roof of buildings looking
towards the city. I thought nothing of
it, just some people gazing at the
picturesque skyline of Manhattan. I
kept listening to my CD player unaware
that the Twin Towers were burning.

When I got off of the train and stepped
out of the station, people were
crowding the streets. I looked up at
the sky and saw smoke. I just thought a
nearby store was on fire. When I walked
into the Wiz store everyone was
surrounding the big screen TV's on
display. They were all tuned to CNN and
had the image of both Towers with smoke
billowing out of it.

I thought it was a movie. I saw my
manager with tears in his eyes. I had
to ask someone if it was real. I stared
at the screen in disbelief for a few
minutes and left the store. I could not

go back in the train station. Every bus that passed was packed. Luckily I remembered how to get back to Brooklyn on the bus from my bowling days at Van Wyck lanes.

I tried to call my loved ones and the lines were dead. Everyone was thinking the same thing. I walked for blocks away from the chaos until I finally found a bus stop where I could get on the bus.

How did this happen? People had transistor radios tuned to 1010WINS and other news stations trying to learn more about what was going on.

To think I just walked through the ground floor of the Towers on the way to the subway 10 days earlier on my birthday with my future wife. It was the end of a nice dinner and walk through Battery Park. I had seen the Towers up close only once before during a field trip with my Art class a year earlier when I was attending L.I.U. My class stood in the plaza between the two buildings and I made the mistake of trying to look up at how tall the Towers were. I almost fell backwards. As I saw it the Towers were colossal.

It was hard to believe buildings this tall and powerful could be felled by terrorists.

Who knew that stroll would be the last time I saw the inside of the Towers?

I will never forget that day, nor will I forget the people who died and those who died trying to save lives. If I would have been off that day I probably would have did what I did once I finally got home: popped a tape in the VCR and record the news coverage. I can't remember if YouTube existed then, but click the link below to see news footage from different networks of that fateful morning.

God Bless America!

http://www.huffingtonpost.com/2011/09/09/911-tv-coverage_n_940613.html#s339292&title=NBC_Live_Coverage

Posted by Jamiyl Samuels at 7:45 PM

Friday September 30, 2011

The Low End Theory 20 Years Later

On September 24, 1991 my favorite Hip Hop album of all time (arguably Tribe's best) was released. Two cassette tapes and one CD later I am still bumping **"Verses From The Abstract"**, **"Buggin' Out"**, **"Jazz (We Got)"**, and **"Vibes And Stuff"** among other gems from this classic, this masterpiece of REAL Hip Hop skill and production.

20 years later *The Low End Theory*, the second album from **A Tribe Called Quest**, still stands the test of time,

reborn for a new generation by actor
Michael Rappaport's documentary **Beats,
Rhymes and Life**. No one before Tribe
fused jazz music with Hip Hop
so deftly, so flawlessly. It made me
wanna learn how to play bass guitar.
Although many believe the follow-
up **Midnight Marauders** is Tribe's magnum
opus, though a close second, I beg to
differ. **Low End** broke barriers, set
trends, took chances creatively when
rappers weren't worried about record
sales and label executives weren't
pressuring rappers to conform to what
was hot.

You heard Q-Tip laughing on track,
stumbling over words in the intro
to **"Verses"** and it was all there. You
felt like you were in the studio with
Tribe when they were cutting their
records and that authenticity made them
more down to earth.

Low End paved the way for
Guru's **Jazzmatazz** series, songs
like **"Props Over Here"**by
the **Beatnuts** and groups like **The
Roots** and their **Do You Want More** album.
Hopefully the group can get back
together and deliver that final album
they owe Jive Records. The game needs a

legitimate throwback.

What tiga What tiga What tiga What tiga
What tiga What tiga What tiga WHAT?!?!

Posted by Jamiyl Samuels at 10:32 AM

Monday November 7, 2011

Magic, 20 Years Later

Today (Nov. 7th) is the 20th
anniversary of the day the sports world
was rocked by Los Angeles Lakers
superstar **Magic Johnson**'s announcement

219

that he would be retiring
from basketball because he
contracted **HIV**, the virus that
causes **AIDS**.

I, like evryone else was stunned by the
news. He had just made the NBA Finals a
few months before losing to **Michael
Jordan** and the Bulls (the one time I
ever rooted for Chicago to win because
I was tired of the Lakers being in the
Finals every year). His startling
announcement shed new light on what was
thought to be a "gay disease". HIV and
AIDS were thought to be the same thing
at the time so many people believed
Magic was going to die. Many of the
players in the NBA were uneducated
about the disease and thus when Magic
attempted to return to basketball a few
months later, he was met with an
ignorance and fear by some of the
superstar players in the league, most
notably **Karl Malone**, that made him
reconsider and stay retired.

Malone, erroneously thinking the virus
could be spread through sweat,
expressed his concern stating he would
not play as hard if he knew someone who
had the virus was playing. Cleveland
all-star guard **Mark Price** was another

outspoken player and, if I remember correctly, **Charles Barkley** was fearful as well.

Magic Johnson's press conference that day was classic Magic. Although he was probably scared out of his mind, he managed to step up to the microphone and tell the world why he decided he would leave the game he loved and dominated. It had to be tough, his wife Cookie sitting to his right pregnant with their child (both Cookie and the future Earvin Johnson, Jr. tested negative), Commissioner David Stern, and the recently retired Kareem Abdul Jabbar, who shared all of those championship moments with Magic in the '80s, to his left. Still Magic was able to flash his trademark smile as he told a captive audience that he would live on and go on with his life. The fierce competitior that he was, Magic was not going to let HIV defeat him.

As inspiring as his positive attitude that day was, his triumphant return to the court in February of 1992 for the NBA All-Star game was just as uplifting. Magic, on the ballot because he was an active player at the start of the '91-'92 season, was voted a starter by the fans even though he did not play a game that season and he more than delivered. All I remember about the game was the high-fives he received from his West teammates (even Malone) during the announcement of the All-stars and the end of the game where he was guarded by former good friend Isiah Thomas and Michael Jordan on consecutive possessions. These matchups got a huge rise out of the crowd, but when Magic hit an off balance 3-point shot on Thomas, the 42 points he scored and game MVP he won was the perfect exclamation point to a Hall of Fame career ended too soon.

Magic also started the **Magic Johnson Foundation** that fateful day effectively becoming the face of HIV in a "if it could happen to Magic, it could happen to anyone" sort of way. Johnson used his platform to educate not only the NBA and its players about the difference between HIV and AIDS and how the HIV virus could be transmitted, but kids, adults, people who were ignorant to the facts about the epidemic that would become a pandemic.

The "cut rule" was introduced into the NBA that season. If a player suffered an open wound or if blood was drawn during play a time out was immediately called so that team doctor could stop the bleeding before play resumed.

Magic was in the prime of his career when he stepped away, all of 32 years old. Although he did manage to comeback late in the '95-'96 season, the game had already changed. All of his former teammates had retired or moved on to other teams and the young players on the roster did not mix well with the aging star. Magic retired for good after that season and has actually gained weight since his playing days leading artists like Kanye West to playfully rap that Magic has the cure for AIDS.

If he does I can't think of a better man who is more deserving.

Below is a surprise appearance Magic made on **The Arsenio Hall show** (throwback!) the day after losing to Jordan and the Bulls in the 1991 Finals. Check out how classy he is in defeat.

https://www.youtube.com/watch?feature=player_embedded&v=fW_csrmx5-U

Then five months later having to do this:

https://www.youtube.com/watch?feature=player_embedded&v=iSfy4AhDDnw

Friday November 18, 2011

Heavy D laid to rest today

☐Hip Hop's "Overweight Lover" and first big man sex symbol will be laid to rest today (Nov. 18th) at Grace Baptist Church in Mount Vernon. In honor of the "Heavster" I have compiled a bunch of my favorite videos from Heav D below.

May you have a peaceful journey, my brother.

Please go to this site to see my selection of classic Hip Hop from Dwight "Heavy D" Myers. Have a Peaceful Journey.

224

http://www.wreachavoconline.blogspot.com/2011
/11/heavy-d-laid-to-rest-today.html?m=1

Posted by Jamiyl Samuels at 11:38 AM

New book "Pass The Torch" is
available today!

**"Pass The Torch: How A Young Black
Father Challenges The 'Deadbeat Dad'
Stereotype"** is now available at the
Createspace.com e-
store.https://www.createspace.com/35666
86

Not only does the book speak on my
experience as a victim of an absentee
father, it analyzes the theme of
fatherhood in controversial films *"Boyz*

225

N Da Hood", *"Menace II Society"*,
and *"He Got Game"*, Fathers in Hip Hop,
the absence of the Black family sitcom
and more.

Please support Black fatherhood by
ordering your copy today!

You can also order from Amazon.com
here: http://www.amazon.com/Pass-Torch-
Challenges-Deadbeat-
Stereotype/dp/0615484425/ref=sr_1_1?s=b
ooks&ie=UTF8&qid=1321645342&sr=1-1

Posted by Jamiyl Samuels at 11:12 AM

226

ABOUT THE AUTHOR

Jamiyl Samuels has been creative writing for over 25 years. Whether it is screenwriting, making numerous contributions to entertainment magazines, blogs and websites as a freelance writer, creating poetry or song lyrics, Samuels continues to do what he loves while striving to make an impact with his work.

He graduated with a Bachelor's degree in English and a Master's degree in Media Arts with a concentration in screenwriting from Long Island University in Brooklyn, New York.

He is the founder of W.R.E.a.C Havoc Enterprises, a company that fosters growth, creativity and education through informed written content, film, and recorded music.

He is currently working on his latest novel and growing his small business online. He resides in New York with his wife and two children.

Read Jamiyl's daily thoughts on his blog at www.wreachavoconline.blogspot.com